The Whole Forest for a Backyard

The Whole Forest for a Backyard:
A Gunflint Trail Wilderness Memoir

Timothy McDonnell

NORTH STAR PRESS OF ST. CLOUD, INC.
St. Cloud, Minnesota

For my parents, Pat and Bette McDonnell,
and for my beloved Maggie.

ISBN: 978-0-87839-646-7

This is a work of nonfiction. Some of the names have been altered in deference to privacy.

First Edition, June 2013

Printed in the United States of America

Published by
North Star Press of St. Cloud, Inc.
St. Cloud, Minnestoa

Table of Contents

Our Creator would never have made such lovely days, and have given us the deep hearts to enjoy them, above and beyond all thought, unless we were meant to be immortal.
Nathanial Hawthorne

Detours on the Road North

here must be a special legion of angels assigned just to watch over travelers and idiots. Somehow I have reached the age of fifty-six years when by rights I should have become crow bait on this wilderness road a long time ago. More than once here I was forced to hitch a ride to the nearest telephone to call a friend or family member and arrange for my car to be dislodged from a snowbank. Most of my experiences with this road predate the invention of cell phones, which, as many a frustrated tourist could attest, do not work in these woods anyway. That stretch between the North Brule Bridge and Swamper Lake always was particularly lousy with moose in the winter. I remember narrowly missing a bull down on its front knees licking road salt not long after I purchased my first car. My Volkswagen and I did a complete pirouette when I hit the brakes. Only a hand from above kept me from crashing into Bullwinkle, the ditch, or another vehicle. That moose just gave me a bewildered stare and did not bother to rise to his feet.

Probably the stupidest thing I ever did on this road was ride a bicycle from town twenty-some miles to meet up with a friend at Aspen Annie's Bar long after the sun had set. I had no light, no reflective clothing, and not the sense God gave a goose. Nope, this road owes me nothing. So, on my last trip up this road, I did not mind at all being someone else's angel.

My packed car with the kayak on the roof rack might easily have marked me as a tourist, for my rig looked similar to scores of others in the heavy summer traffic. It seemed the majority of vehicles had either a canoe or a kayak up top. By contrast, the pickup truck that had pulled way over on the road shoulder had all the markings of belonging to a local. The tailgate was down. It was about half full of firewood logs. Chainsaw and gas can were set in one corner of the truck bed. A man and a woman clad in work clothes were franticly waving. I pulled over and turned on my hazard lights before noticing the dead deer on the pavement. They had just collided with this animal, trashing both it and the truck's radiator in the process. They wanted the favor of a ride to the telephone at Trail Center. When I learned they had a summer home on West Bearskin Lake, I did them one better and dropped them off at their front door. It felt good to help these two, and for a while I thought of myself as being once again a local in this wilderness.

Leaving the gravel of the Clearwater Road, I hit pavement once more near the Forest Service sign marking the 1967 Hungry Jack Lake Fire. The pines all along here came back thick and close together, as if with a vengeance. I knew, were it not for that sign, many people would never notice that over 800 acres had burned. I understood that fire is a must for the spruce and jack pine in this wilderness, for their serotinous cones require intense heat in order to pop open and disperse seeds for regeneration. I understood that fire prepares the forest floor for renewal. Somehow my knowing this never made it any easier to look out upon any stretch of burnt wilderness. As I drove on, I thought about how troublesome it has been for me to accept fire as a positive force vital to the perpetuation of this forest I love as I love no other place on earth.

Smokey Bear's pointer at the rescue squad garage near Poplar Lake indicated a low risk of fire. There had been a lot of rain the previous week. Puddles were everywhere. Paddling in the rain did not worry me much. However, there were a few of my old haunts I wanted to revisit, and rain would not make that any easier. I took a right at the next junction and returned once again to the time when I was not just another tourist here.

I pulled into the parking lot adjacent to the short portage between Hungry Jack Lake and West Bearskin Lake. It took some fifteen miles of driving just to go from the cabin belonging to the stranded woodcutters to this spot because skirting lakes forces the route to be circuitous. Paddling distance from their dock at the end of West

Bearskin to this portage was less than four miles. I began to wonder if I should have stayed and accepted the beer the two woodcutters had offered in gratitude. Launching my kayak from their property would have been easy enough. Such second-guessing was nothing new to me, neither was my choosing solitude over being social. I concluded that the couple would be plenty busy dealing with tow truck logistics. Besides, I was headed for the opposite end of the portage.

God forgot to give me any height. I thought about this, as I often did when trying to car-top a kayak or a canoe single-handedly. A white, folding stepladder became standard equipment in my car years ago. Maybe my system did look a bit goofy. Nonetheless, it always worked, and this day there was no one around to scoff. I gathered what little gear I needed, put my hearing aids into a waterproof case in the pocket of my life jacket, and portaged across to Hungry Jack Lake.

The water was calm. Two boys were fishing just a short distance from shore, and I watched as one pulled in a nice small mouth bass. My fly rod was back at the car, but I had no regrets. The purpose of this detour had nothing to do with fishing. Once this side trip was finished, my plan was to head back out to the paved road and drive on up to my sister's home near its end. I knew there would be time enough later to find a promising spot in her neck of the woods where the fish might cooperate. I waved to the two boys when they looked my way but did not engage them in conversation. With most of my hearing gone, communication on the water without my amplification was at best a frustrating process of repetitions and attempts made to try and fill in the blanks with context clues. I just did not need the hassle, and I imagined they did not need it either. There was nothing churlish in my intent. I learned long ago that it is not always necessary to try to improve upon silence.

It felt good to be on the water once more. Most of my kayaking for the past decade took place on Lake Superior. To trade my wetsuit for a pair of shorts and a tee shirt on this warm inland lake was liberating. Long strokes with a lot of torso rotation helped take away the stiffness brought about by too much time spent behind the wheel. I looked out across Hungry Jack Lake to a rise on the south shore known locally as Mount Anna. The fire of 1967 swept up the backside of this rise. Crews fighting this blaze bulldozed a fuel break between Mount Anna and a nearby home. Had it not been for their quick efforts coupled with a fortunate turn in the weather, the fire would have surely consumed that home and might easily have continued burning up the entire southwest side of the lake. Though there were scars on the land long afterward, crews managed to contain the fire without loss of life or loss of structure.

As I paddled west, the floodgates of my memory opened fully, and I was soon awash in the remembrances of the people and events of my boyhood. All of my earliest recollections of joy had their origins here. Summer homes dotted the shoreline to my right, and for a while I played a happy game trying to recall just who had lived in each of these cabins so long ago. Some connections were easy and unmistakable. I recognized several of the buildings and knew I had been inside most of them as a kid. Even so, I soon lost track. What startled me was how close together everything appeared. It was as if in my absence time had shrunk all distances. It made me smile to see that a few of the old white pines were still standing. So many of these marvelous giants had elsewhere succumbed to heart rot and toppled. These trees were here long before any of us.

Down the lake a bit, three children were playing on a large swimming raft. I saw them before I could hear them. The largest of the bunch had just done a cannon ball causing the other two to squeal with laughter. I chuckled to think this would have been my brothers and me sometime in the distant past. In my reverie, I pictured my mother. When I was young, she would occasionally leave her kitchen duties for a while and come down to the beach to watch us as we played in the water. I recalled that I had never in my life seen her swim. No matter how hard we pleaded with her to come join us in the water, her answer was always the same.

"I cannot go swimming with you," she would invariably explain. "I have a hole in the knee of my bathing suit."

Two women sat on the shore in deck chairs watching the children's fun and chatting with each other. Behind them was a large sweep of lawn, which looked tidy and well kept. The top of the lawn ended at a bright and neatly arranged cobbled patio. The patio seemed the perfect compliment in color and style to the elegant log building it surrounded. With three levels, large dormers, and plenty of glass facing the water, obviously this was a structure built for comfort and built to impress.

I stayed close to the shore and paddled around the point trying to keep out of the way of the numerous motorboats. This resort was a busy spot. Had anyone cared to notice, I might easily have been accused of trying to give the whole operation the old hairy eyeball. My motivation was merely curiosity. I had not one ounce of disdain. This point and I shared a history, and I was craning my neck trying hard to find some evidence of the place I knew. The first three cabins I passed looked familiar, though somewhat altered and perhaps a bit the worse for wear. There was much activity at the boat dock on the west side of the point, and I steered clear of it. I paddled out a ways and looked back to try and gain a broader view. The main lodge building was impressive and fit the site well. I did sense, however, that the entire property seemed congested and a good deal more built upon than the rustic forest retreat I remembered.

It was difficult for me to try to figure out just how to think about what I was seeing here. I was pleased that the place looked so well cared for and clean. More than anything else, I felt proud of my brother, Tad. He and his son, Jason, had recently finished building the main lodge here. From what I could see, they had done a superb job. It was as much a work of art as a place of lodging. I knew who the owner was, but we had never met. I also knew full well that I owed it to my brother to go to shore and fully explore his craftsmanship. However, I was not yet ready to do so. For the third time that day, I chose to remain quiet and alone.

I began to paddle once more, putting distance between the resort and myself. When I reached the east end of the lake, I stopped and drifted for a while. I was free to make my own choices. I decided that I would continue to hold what I knew and loved about this place in my heart and not allow that to change if at all possible. I decided that I would put what I felt down on paper, for paper has staying power. I decided to try to be happy for the owner of the resort and wish him well if ever we met. I would bear him no ill will. I would offer instead a blessing and a sincere hope that his, the fourth log lodge built on that same site since 1924, would outlast us all and not be cursed by the same sort of fires that obliterated the three previous structures. I then turned, set a fine pace for myself, and headed for the portage.

Rootstock

There was a time when my entire world was only sixty miles long. Through the heart of it ran a narrow ribbon of road called the Gunflint Trail. The trail starts in the village of Grand Marais, Minnesota, on the north shore of Lake Superior. It rises over a saw-tooth ridgeline of granite before plunging deep into the boreal forest. About halfway along this wilderness road is the turnoff to Hungry Jack Lake. I grew up on the shores of Hungry Jack where my parents ran a resort called Gateway Lodge.

In the spring of 1958, just a few months shy of my third birthday, my parents uprooted the family from suburban Chicago and transplanted the entire bunch of us amid a sea of trees. This was indeed alien territory. Mom and Dad were banking everything they had on an effort to fulfill a mutual desire to go into business for themselves. The hospitality industry seemed to them a good match with a strong potential.

My father was an easy man to like. Born in southern Illinois, he was the second son of an Irish immigrant. His father was a dreamer and a seeker, who left the County Monaghan family farm at age nineteen and became a success as a Chicago food broker. Like his father, Dad was loquacious and personable. His talent for connecting with strangers, chatting them up amiably, and within minutes finding a common tie was a characteristic any good innkeeper or host would envy. Dad's Chicago job with the United States Treasury Department provided plenty of security, but little personal satisfaction. He longed to be his own boss.

Dad was not at all what you would call mechanically gifted. I take after him in this regard, as I, too, have five thumbs on each hand. Unlike me, Dad usually knew his limits well and was never slow to ask for help. There is no doubt in my mind that a sizable part of my love of wandering came from my dad. So, too, did a sizable portion of my faith and a large chunk of my passion for wild places.

My mother grew up in a small town in southern Iowa, the third daughter of the co-founder of Hy-Vee grocery stores. A summer internship in retail marketing as a college student had lured her to Chicago, where she eventually met and married Dad. Mom was well on her way toward becoming a superb cook long before our family left Chicago. So much more than a simple meat and potatoes handler, her culinary repertoire has long been vast and imaginative. When called upon to provide a selection of hors d'oeuvres for a large gathering early in her marriage, she impressed her neighbors, satisfied appetites, and won my dad's undying admiration by providing twenty-five unique varieties all from scratch. My father rarely left our dinner table without praising my mother's cooking. Today people often ask me what I think is the best place to eat in Grand Marais. The answer is simple: Mom's house.

Mom liked the idea of putting her kitchen talents to work in a venue of her own. Big city life was beginning to wear on her nerves. She grew disenchanted with Chicago. I suspect that newspaper stories of gang violence made her fearful of raising her own boys there. The Big Piney Woods seemed a safer, saner environment. One way or another, her progeny were destined to become free-range children.

From Mom I inherited more than a full measure of stubborn perseverance. It is because of my stubbornness that I will either solve a problem independently or gummy it up beyond all recognition before finally seeking assistance. It is to my eternal regret that I never inherited my mother's sound judgment. However, God has blessed me bountifully, for I did inherit from both of my parents a deep commitment to happiness.

When my parents bought Gateway Lodge in 1958, it was a grand, rustic showplace. It was a true gem from a bygone era, a slower-paced time when people of means sought rejuvenation and would retreat to the wild annually for weeks at a time. The main lodge was built during the Great Depression from white pine logs harvested nearby and dragged to the building site by draft horses. It replaced a far simpler lodge building that had been destroyed in a fire supposedly caused by a careless smoker who had chosen to use the concave handle of a wood box for an ashtray. In their efforts to rebuild, the original owners, Sue and Jesse Gapen, set out to create a masterpiece that became the premier resort in the area. It was in its day the longest full log structure in the state. All of the furniture pieces and much of the décor were made by hand on site from diamond willow, spruce, cedar, birch bark, and tanned deer hide. Surrounded by deep pine forests and more lakes than a person could explore in a lifetime, here was a place that could meet the challenge of my parents' dreams.

Mom and Dad became captives enticed by the romance of this wild place when they signed the purchase agreement. It was all so fresh, so green, and so different from Chicago life. So strong was the pull that practicality took a back seat to dreaming. Although the lodge had running water and electricity, there was not one toilet anywhere on the nine-acre property. The construction of a central bathhouse for the lodge and a full bathroom for our cabin home would be top priorities. My parents were rich in outhouses and mighty grateful that at the time of purchase only one of their children was in diapers. With a healthy dose of optimism and a great deal of hard work, they modernized the rental cabins, winterized our cabin home, built a reputation for excellent dining, and instilled a deep love of wilderness in each of their six kids.

My parents' primary charge as resort owners was to ensure their guests were all well fed, relaxed, and happy enough to come back for another vacation next season. Mom and Dad excelled in this. I witnessed first hand the high regard returning families held for our place in the woods. People with the means to vacation just about anywhere chose to return to Gateway Lodge summer after summer. I knew we had something special here. I understood that I was indeed a blessed and lucky child, for I came from good rootstock and had the whole forest for a backyard.

As a rule, my five siblings and I see ourselves as being fiercely independent. We are not a people of small opinions. We tend to be largely unfamiliar with backing down and are more than a little proud of our individual differences. Unique as we may appear, scratch the surface on any one of us and what you will find is a common passion. Each of the lot of us has at the core an inextricable love for the same forest home to which we are all rooted.

While my siblings and I perceive this core love of the wilderness as fundamental to who we are, it is not universally understood or even acknowledged among my relatives. Take as an example this recent comment from one of my uncles.

"I don't know how your folks ever managed in that tiny house in that godforsaken wilderness with all you kids," he shared.

My wife and I were sitting in my uncle's kitchen in suburban Chicago when he let loose with that sentiment. I was stung, for his words cut to the bone. I kept silent. Not for the world would I willingly hurt this man. Still, how could this uncle of mine, my own godfather, not know what this wilderness was and still is to my family and to me?

It is unlikely that my uncle was alone in his view of my parents' choice to raise a family where they did. In retrospect, I admire the courage, the faith, and the love it took for Mom and Dad to plunge into a totally new way of life. They were indeed babes in the woods when they began. God never has forsaken these woods nor those who chose to make it their home. All these many years later, I can think of no finer place on earth to be a small boy with a large imagination.

These days I am a bit of an anomaly amid my clan of vocal individualists. I am the partially deaf one who relishes silence. Attending to silence in a wilderness setting has taught me a thing or two over the years, and I was raised to always share a good thing. I have learned that happiness is a renewable resource. I have learned that contentment flourishes in the natural world. My ability to tap into this joy depends less on what I bring for my journey than what I jettison.

Geez, Look at the Trees

The lack of billboards may not be the first thing a traveler heading up the Gunflint Trail notices, but I have always found their absence refreshing. Nothing gets in the way of the views. The trees welcome and envelop. In place of the garish intrusions typical of highway advertising, you will find neat, uniform sets of ladder signs. The area resort owners and canoe outfitters banded together decades ago, formed a collaboration called the Gunflint Trail Association, and created these signs in a spirit of cooperation. The name of the business and the distance to its front door are all each sign slat will tell you. The rest you get to discover for yourself. Five or six slats are hung from the log framework of each ladder sign. These are placed strategically along the trail, and they serve as simple, helpful and unobtrusive mileage markers. They are also symbolic of the neighborly, cooperative spirit of the locals here; people who make their livelihoods connecting visitors with the myriad lakes and the forest surrounding them. These are folks who know how to share a good thing. In doing so, their intentions are the same as my own. Awareness leads to appreciation. Appreciation will hopefully lead to the preservation of what is mutually shared and mutually loved.

I do not claim to have a proprietary relationship with these woods. To do so goes against my nature. I cannot own a section of the sky and say that cloud is mine. The sky is constantly changing. So, too, is the water. What manner of fool stakes a claim on a certain set of waves? This forest is likewise an ever-altering environment transforming at a pace all its own. Some of the stately white pine giants encountered along the Gunflint Trail and along a few of the side roads are more than three centuries old. These trees do evoke a certain sense of permanence until fire and straight-line winds char and topple them. I embody my own set of transformations and am both rooted and transient. I am a part of this forest and at the same time apart from it.

Try as I may, I cannot recall a time when I did not know these woods. They are constant enough for me. The ladder signs continue to show me how far I have come and how far I have yet to go. To find the turnoff to the Hungry Jack Lake Road, start counting the miles after the second set of ladder signs. It is pretty hard to miss. To find Gateway Lodge, take a right at the turnoff and travel back about half a century.

It is funny how distances contract over time. Take for example this gravel road stretching from the macadam of the Gunflint Trail, past the trailhead to Caribou Rock with its fine stand of portal pines, and at last down to the lodge itself. I remember well trudging up these same hills going from the lodge out to our mailbox on the trail with my brother, Chris, one long ago January Saturday. The road seemed endless, an eternal uphill slog.

Chris was born a year and two weeks after me. In our early years, we were closer to being twins than anything else. Mom and Dad usually gave us identical Christmas presents each year. They gave us the identical Royal Racer sleds we pulled up these interminable hills. We were hardy trappers, mountain men, intrepid mushers rushing the serum to Nome and destined to become heroes. We sneered at hardship, laughed in the face of death, and spat in the eye of every polar bear we encountered. Then we got cold.

Chris and I encouraged each other and tried to remember that we were doing this for fun. The two miles seemed to zip right by in the early school day mornings aboard the bus Dad drove to Grand Marais. This, however, was climbing the Matterhorn with Mount Everest piled on top for good measure while each of us pulled a mile long freight train. We tried to keep our focus on the downhill return home. Once the road flattened out near Road Lake, we ran to warm ourselves.

Mail time was usually an opportunity for locals to gather and jaw a bit. In the middle of January, though, the only other local was Walt from across Hungry Jack Lake. Walt was a world champion gossip and a bit of an old crank. His was one of the other telephone numbers on our party line, and he used to listen in on everyone else's conversations. You could sometimes hear him breathing or clearing his throat. We were not sure he would stoop to chat with a couple of half-frozen McDonnell boys, and I felt a bit of relief to find his car was nowhere to be seen. No one else was at the mailboxes. There were no fresh tire tracks, and we had received a light coating of snow since Mr. Staples had come down the road with the county plow truck. I pulled the old pillowcase from my parka pocket, collected the mail, and was pleased there were no large packages to contend with. Then came the fun part.

Soon the two of us were in position at the crest of the long hill near the gravel pit. We almost forgot the cold in our anticipation and bravado.

"Betcha I can get all the way to Leo Creek before stopping," Chris challenged.

"No fair dragging your feet in the turns. If you wipe out, you lose," I replied. I had the mailbag tucked in between my parka and my sweater. "You go first. You're fun to watch."

"Good bye, cruel world!" Chris hollered. With that he was off, picking up speed. I could hear him let out a few wild whoops before he turned out of sight.

My turn now. I pulled down on my balaclava and pulled up on my parka collar. I made sure the towrope was under my belly where it would not get caught in the sled runners.

"Here goes nothing!" Almost at once my eyes blurred with tears in the rush of cold air. It was no longer any surprise to me that downhill skiers wore those goofy looking goggles. I thought about how goofy I would look wearing my swim mask, and then wished I had it. The snow was hard-packed and smooth, perfect for sledding.

"I gotta keep my feet up," I reminded myself. Then there would be more of a chance of making it past that long flat stretch between hills by Leo Lake without stopping. As much as possible, I tried to follow the tracks Chris left behind. There was no salt or grit sand on this snowy road. If you could not make it up these hills in winter back then, you and your car either stayed home or learned all about fighting the tire chain demons.

The wind was wicked. No doubt Chris would have given me grief about crying if he had seen my face. Of course, his eyes had blurred up, too. I thought if I only had just a little more speed, momentum would take me to the next hill. I slowed a bit right before coming to the crest. Then I was on my way.

"Yee-haw!"

I coursed through a bit of an S curve and then came barreling down the hill by the turnoff to Walt's place. That was exactly where Dad sent me airborne the winter I was five when he got the crazy notion to pull us kids on the toboggan hitched to the station wagon. I was the only kid riding as Dad came down the hill and gunned the engine so the toboggan would not hit his back bumper. I went flying and landed in a snow bank. Mom thought I was dead, pulled me out of the snow, and called a permanent halt to such foolish fun. I wondered what she would have thought of our sledding and figured it was just as well she was not watching. It was a good thing we had no traffic to contend with on the road in the winter.

Then I saw Chris. He was almost at a dead stop, and he was trying to inch his sled a little bit farther on sheer willpower. I pulled in right beside him. We were a bit less than twenty yards from where the culvert for Leo Creek runs under the road.

"Pretty darn close," I gave him.

"Close enough," he returned. "I was going to hurry and pull my sled right up to the culvert and flop back down on it again, but you were right on my tail."

From where we stopped, Hungry Jack Lake was visible through the trees. The road curved around to the north side of the lake. Gateway Lodge was on a prominent point jutting out from the north shore. We had a bit more walking to do before reaching the portal pines and making our last run down the long hill to the lodge.

I love these fine old pines. In my mind, they served as the gateway to my family's home in the woods. Upon reaching them in days long gone, I knew I was safely back in the shelter of my family's love.

Today many of these same old pines remain, and they welcome just as they have always done. This road is still gravel. However, it is much more heavily used. Two small boys riding sleds from the top of the long hill near the gravel pit down to where the culvert for Leo Creek runs under the road would be asking for trouble dodging cars and snowmobiles the whole way down. Total quiet along this road is a rare occurrence these days even in winter. It only takes a few minutes to travel the distance from the macadam of the Gunflint Trail out by the mailboxes to the resort that now stands where Gateway Lodge once stood. It is a short distance that reminds me of all we have gained and all we have lost in the past half-century. Sled run or no sled run, I find my eyes still water and blur from time to time these days.

Of Root Beer Bellies and One-Button Shirts

he beauty of being raised in a wilderness setting is that there is infinite potential for the development of a keen play ethic. The beauty of being raised in a large family is that you almost always have a playmate. Both factors proved invaluable, living as we did thirty-two miles from town. We made our own fun, and we were good at it. Mom and Dad gave us a great deal of freedom tempered with what turned out to be just the right amount of responsibility.

For most of my family's tenure at Gateway Lodge, I was the middle child with two older siblings and two younger. In mid-August of 1965, we were blessed with the arrival of my brother, Pat, the final child of the brood. Well before Pat's arrival, Chris and I had the joys of summer figured out pretty well. We were lodge brothers, and we knew how to make the most of that.

Summer garb for Chris and for me typically included a pair of shorts, which doubled as swim trunks, and a pair of Red Ball Jet sneakers. As often as not, the Jets were on the wrong feet and the laces were a tangled snarl of knots. The buttonholes of any shirt Chris put on seldom aligned perfectly with the row of buttons. I chuckle these days to see young fellows walking around with their trousers at half-mast. Chris had the droopy drawers look mastered decades ago due to his lack of hips. To this day, he grimaces at the memory of unbidden grown-ups grabbing hold of the waist of his sagging shorts trying to reassemble him with the words: "Hey, little partner, your shirt and shorts don't meet." This was seldom an issue for me. Usually my shirt was still in the drawer, left down on the beach, or was collecting dust bunnies under my bunk bed. More often than not, I wore what Dad called my one-button shirt.

If any one of us kids was within whistling distance of Mom or Dad when newly arrived guests checked in at the lodge office, our play could be put on hold. We might be summoned for guide duty and asked to show folks around the lodge property. Mom's whistle was a subtle three shorts and a long. We all knew that it meant come hither. Dad had a sharp, piercing whistle that could make a fellow's hair stand on end. I have never been able to replicate it, though my older brother, Jack, once talked me into trying to do so with a mouthful of crackers. The result was entirely what he had anticipated right down to my fetching the broom and dustpan. There was no mistaking that Dad's whistle meant business. It had an attitude all its own.

Guide duty became a part of my life at an early age and was never entirely separate from play. Once when I was about five, I proudly pointed out the key features of our beach and boat dock area to a nice older couple. Walking up to one of the watercraft, I put my hand on it and said, "This one here is our square-stern canoe. Do you got a square stern, lady?"

To which the gentleman chuckled and replied, "She sure does, Sonny."

If Dad's shrill whistle or Mom's subtle three shorts and a long had conjuring powers, just where would this shirtless five-year-old boy with his summer tan and his root beer belly lead a visitor? The typical tour always began in the lodge office. Often the aroma of fresh-baked bread drifted in from the nearby kitchen making the guests want to linger a bit. We passed through handmade double doors and into the dining room. Here the exposed log beams always made me think of the hull of a great wooden ship turned upside-down. The ridgepole, or the keel as I imagined it, was 126 feet long and ran the full length of the building. Just about everything in the dining room was handcrafted using local materials. This included all the tables and chairs, the buffet cupboards and the two large curio cabinets, even the candleholders and all the light fixtures. The beams and log walls of the dining room were well varnished and highly polished. When the sunlight streamed through the windows at just the right angle, all this wood had a pleasant, almost magical glow.

Next we would go down the huge split log steps into the lounge. Guests would gaze about taking in the armchairs, sofas, side tables, floor lamps, bookshelves, and the terrific twin writing desks all of which were fashioned by hand from wood and bark native to the area. Folks were always impressed by the large grandfather clock in the lounge. This, too, was made on site.

The interior of the lodge was a taxidermist's dream. On the walls were mounted trophy fish and rugs made from the skins of wolves, bobcats, and black bears. The bear rugs always fascinated folks. The plastic teeth in the mouths looked so savage and frightening. I would not have been terribly surprised if out of those synthetic jaws came the words: "Back off boy or you're gonna be lunch." On the mantle above the fireplace in the lounge was a stuffed snowy owl. Nearby on one of the log purlins, a stuffed pileated woodpecker was mounted in perpetual mid-strike. A perceptive visitor might feel he or she had stepped into a place that was part arts-and-crafts museum and part preserved menagerie. All the while, the less than perceptive pipsqueak guide would continue to chatter away like a red squirrel.

Though I have never been a huge fan of taxidermy, it had its place and its purpose at Gateway. Often these stuffed representations were the first encounters guests had of the woodland creatures indigenous to the area. In the dining room on opposite ends of the mantle above that fireplace were mounted twin bear cubs. These were popular and caught the eye and the interest of most visitors. When asked how the little cubbies were acquired, the standard reply was that they had been discovered drowned and were given to the original lodge owners, who had them stuffed. This usually satisfied the curious. Whether or not that is the truth of the matter, I cannot say. I know that I was convinced enough as a child to give this same reply dozens of times to inquiring visitors. The fact that bears are excellent swimmers was entirely overlooked.

If I could go back in time and once again conduct a nickel tour of Gateway Lodge, I would include all of my favorite play haunts as well as the several working parts of my family's business. There was much the typical lodge guest never got to experience. For example, they missed out on the cool, dank, earthy smells of the root cellar. Here a little boy could pretend he was a caveman or a leprechaun. There might even be a pot of gold somewhere in one of the dark corners. More likely, a treasure seeker here would come across the very first spud ever tossed into the bin.

Guests were never shown the lodge's large stone incinerator. This was where all our cardboard boxes went to die. Just up the hill from this was the vent shaft for the root cellar. By removing the cover and shouting down into the shaft, you could create some great echoes.

Of course, on such an elaborate tour, a side trip through the kitchen for a cookie or three would be a must. To me, the kitchen was the heart of the lodge, and Mom was the heart of the kitchen. I can see her clearly standing in front the massive, black kitchen range. She was ever the master of organizing a fine, full meal for a crowd. She usually had at least three things cooking at once, and would be thinking ahead to the next three to be prepared. In addition, Mom did all the baking for the lodge. We were never a Wonder Bread family. The cookie jar for lodge and family was an antique glass container from some old apothecary shop, and on it was the label "FOLLY CATHARTIC TABLETS." That seems fitting. To this day, I will swear by the medicinal qualities of my mother's oatmeal chocolate chip cookies.

Right above Mom's range was a giant peaked skylight. Whenever rain hit this, as it often did in early summer storms, the entire kitchen sounded like a snare drum.

While the guests were still in the office registering, Dad would explain that every cabin rental included three meals each day served in the dining room. In the days of the lodge's original owner, guests were summoned to the dining room with a bugle call. The battered old brass bugle hung from a peg on the wall near the office. Try as we may, none of us could make more than an atonal *blat* with the thing. My parents used a large cast iron school bell affixed to a two-by-eight plank on the corner of the lodge to announce meal times. If I was around the kitchen at the right time and one step ahead of my siblings, I got to ring the bell when Mom gave the word.

Although most guests did not enter the kitchen, they frequently gathered nearby on the large stone patio directly in front of the lodge. This was a comfortable setting with stone benches and Adirondack chairs. The lodge had a circular driveway, and the patio was in the middle of this circle partly surrounded by gardens. A thick bank of ferns on one side made an excellent place for hide-and-go-seek until your little brothers caught on to you. Guests often read and relaxed on the patio or fed peanuts to the local tribe of chipmunks. These little creatures were not exactly wild, nor were they the least bit timid in their begging. On the contrary, as the summer progressed, so, too, did their boldness and the size of their back haunches.

I have no clear recollection of what exactly enticed me to try and turn a somersault on this stone patio when I was three, but I remember the aftermath quite well. I left the chipmunks and ran into the lodge kitchen crying with both hands on top of my head. My sister, Kath, tried to console me and to assure me that I was all right and should just go back outside and play. She was Mom's helper in the kitchen and understood better than any of the rest of us kids just how busy Mom was. However, when I put my hands down and turned toward Mom, both could see the blood streaming from the back of my head. I had landed hard, splitting my scalp and necessitating an emergency trip to town. For a few days afterward, I wore my stitches like a crown bowing my head and showing them off to any lodge guests who looked my way.

Just beyond the stone patio was the waterfront with our beach and our boat docks. This is where my little brothers and I spent most of our time playing. This is where every lodge guest eventually gravitated not long after arrival. Most lodge guests came for the fishing. In fact, it was the combination of excellent fishing opportunities and relief from hay fever that prompted the original owners to create a resort business here in the first place. At age five, I knew nothing about hay fever, but I could talk your ear off about fishing for bluegills. Most lodge guests were after finny critters far larger than the dock crib quarry my brothers and I mastered. Inevitably, guests would ask Dad at check in time how the fish were biting. Just as inevitably, came his reply: "Oh, you should have been here last week."

During our first few lodge summers, Mom was more concerned about us kids getting impaled by fishhooks than she was about our being around water. There were usually plenty of people around the boat docks and beach area to keep us out of any serious trouble. When Chris was three and I was four, we fished with bottle openers tied to hand lines. By age five, we had graduated to real hooks and were digging our own worms.

Bluegills are not the smartest of fish. We would catch dozens of these through the slat cracks of the main boat dock. We sometimes collected them in a bucket of lake water for a while just to see how many we could catch. If lodge guests had kids, they soon became our fishing pals. Before long, we would all be sharing from the same worm can and peering down through the slat cracks with our butts in the air. We always let the fish go and could not imagine anyone eating a bluegill. They were our buddies. Either these fish were in limitless numbers, or a small handful of bluegills had rubber lips and alarmingly poor memories. I was never certain which.

Though Chris and I were catch-and-release fishermen, there was one tiny fish he did harvest. He placed it under his bed pillow. It could be that he completely misunderstood the Tooth Fairy's curriculum vitae. Perhaps he figured the tiny fish would be a ten-pound walleye when he woke in the morning. Then he would be a real fisherman like big brother Jack. Mom caught wind of this—actually, we all did before long—and Chris went back to letting go all he hooked.

At just about the center point of the lodge property and fairly sheltered by trees were three outbuildings most of the guests knew nothing about. Each of these structures provided a great place for a little boy to play and pretend. The smallest and by far messiest of these was the old powerhouse where a fellow could imagine he was Reddy Kilowatt. This sheltered a diesel generator unit, which we no longer used. The Cook County chapter of the Rural Electric Association had hooked Gateway up to the grid a short time prior to my parents' purchase of the lodge. Some of the old timers living around the lake would tell our family their recollections of just how loud the generator was once it was fired up in the evening. I heard that it served as an additional signal for a few of the die-hard fisher folk to come in off the water when the onset of darkness by itself was insufficient to do the job.

The largest of the three structures was the ice house. Who needed a sandbox to play in when you had such a mountain of sawdust? If we dug down deep enough, we found chunks of ice that had been harvested from the lake years ago and had never melted. Sawdust is an excellent insulator. Mom's kitchen had a walk-in cooler, and though it had originally been chilled with huge ice blocks, it was retrofitted with an electric refrigeration unit. Dad had installed two freezers on the back porch of the lodge. We no longer needed an ice house, but it was fun to discover how things were done in the long ago.

The third building was a rickety two-stall garage. Chris and I rarely chose this as a place to play, and I recall being a little afraid that the roof would collapse on our heads. We did not need the garage to play in when one of the greatest toys of all our boyhood days rested and rusted just outside the door. This was a derelict Ford Model A flatbed truck. With a couple of boat cushions atop the bench seat to keep the popped springs from tearing into our fannies, the two of us cruised the backwoods of our imaginations. We were a couple of outlaw speed demons on the lookout for the Gunflint Trail cops. We kept an eye pealed for humongous bull moose or ginormous black bears to run over. Anytime we felt we were running low on gas, one of us would bail out and dash over to the ice house for a handful of sawdust. This would go down the fuel pipe. When we really got going, we pretended the engine was just about to blow sky high. This necessitated a loud screeching of the brakes, which was done in stereo, of course. Off came the radiator cap. In went a handful of that wonderful multipurpose sawdust. Then, we were back on the road with a mad lurch of the steering wheel and an expert hand on the gear shifter. Lookout all you slowpoke tourists!

My imagined nickel tour would end back in the lodge kitchen. This is where I ended most of my summer day as a boy. When the dining room crowd had at last cleared out and the kitchen had at last calmed down, Dad and Mom usually sat together and had a chat. I loved this quieter time when my parents could relax and simply be Mom and Dad once more. When I fish the recesses of my memory, I can readily pull up the image of me sitting on my dad's lap sharing a stool with him in the lodge kitchen on toward my bed time. He occasionally tousled my crew cut while talking with Mom. Ours was a particularly symbiotic relationship at the time. Trying to unwind, he would take a sip from his Hamm's Beer and I would belch loudly. All too soon, Mom would send me off to bed. I would say good night, leave by the back porch door, and run as fast as I could across the road to our cabin home once more outpacing both the bears and the boogieman.

Homage to George the Bear

eorge S. Wilson, Jr., was an attorney from Owensboro, Kentucky. Though not a particularly large man, he stood as the giant of my boyhood admiration. This fellow was the first non-family member I knew to be a truly good man. He came up to the lodge every summer for two weeks usually staying in cabin #9 on his own, but sometimes he arrived with his wife, Virginia. He was a fine fisherman, a Gateway regular, and a favorite lodge guest. As a favorite, the members of my family always called him by his first name.

The only other George familiar to us kids was the giant bearskin rug that covered a good portion of the floor on one side of the lounge. This behemoth must have been mighty impressive when alive and on the prowl. My older brother, Jack, once crawled under this huge rug, reared up and scared the snot out of me. It took a moment for the opposing concepts to register and for me to recognize that although Jack was not entirely harmless, what was left of this old bruin most certainly was. How this outsized ursus came to be called George remains a mystery.

George the guest became George the Bear early in our friendship. Just why that happened is also a mystery, for he had none of the fearsome qualities of his name source. He was a gentle, kind man, who became our surrogate grandpa. There was no uncertainty regarding the love my family felt for him. The truth is we saw far more of George the Bear than we ever saw of any of our real grandparents and indeed felt closer to him. If I close my eyes, I can easily picture the smile on this fellow's large, square face. His tan jacket is as familiar to me all these years later as any now hanging in my own closet. I can still hear in my mind's ear the slow, melodic drawl of his voice. When he said good morning to you, it took longer than it did for other folks. You knew he meant it, and his greeting always ended in a nod and a lingering smile.

In my memory, George the Bear is seated in the lodge dining room at the table nearest the fireplace. He has just finished breakfast, his predictable two eggs sunny side up and crisp around the edges with bacon and toast made from Mom's fresh baked bread. He sits back and pulls out his pipe and a red pocket tin of Prince Albert tobacco. He chuckles to himself, for he knows all too well that the aroma of his pipe smoke is a signal to a certain trio of little boys. Mealtime is over. Mom and Dad taught us never to cross through the dining room while the guests were eating. No problem now. Tad, Chris, and I sneak up to George the Bear's table from the back way through the lounge.

"When can we all go on our picnic together?" one of us asks, or more likely all three of us ask.

"Tomorrow," he replies.

"But you said that yesterday," we explain in less than genuine dismay. We have played this game before and know it pretty well. George the Bear's response will always be the same: "Tomorrow," until the best day of his whole two week stay when he finally says: "Today."

Picnic day with George the Bear was always a summer highlight, and I remember fondly the first picnic day that included Tad as well as Chris and me. Mom supplied us with enough sandwiches, fruit, sliced veggies, cookies, and pop from her kitchen to satisfy a small army. George the Bear handled the outboard, as three little boys filled with excitement and chatter piled into his boat. Together we headed down the lake. I sat on the middle seat with Tad while Chris was up in the bow. My feet were propped against George the Bear's huge tackle box. He had removed the lures from all of his fishing rods lest we perforate ourselves, what with all our squirming.

On our way down the lake, George the Bear entered a back bay not far from the Flour Lake portage. He said he wanted to check out the beaver house here to see if there was any activity. With all the noise that came from a certain three little picnickers, any beavers in the area had to be deaf and blind to be out and about.

George the Bear shut the motor down and we drifted a bit.

"Boys," he said, "look for yellow sticks near the top of the beaver house. Those would be the freshest sticks."

"What about all those gray sticks," I asked, "the ones that look like a bunch of driftwood?"

"Well now, those were yellow once," he replied. "You see, boys, the sun dries those sticks out and they turn from yellow to gray. The beaver makes his supper out of the leaves and the bark of the trees he takes down. Think of the sticks as leftovers. Those are used to make the beaver house stronger. Look at how all that wood is in the water. Do you know why those sticks don't rot?"

"Nope," Chris answered for the three of us.

"Well you see, boys," George the Bear explained, "as old Mr. Beaver is peeling away on the bark and eating, he is coating the wood with saliva. There is something in the saliva that helps keep the wood from rotting."

"What's surviva?" asked Tad.

"Saliva is just a fancy word for spit."

Chris and I immediately looked at each other. We simultaneously faked the launching of rich, giant hawkers over the side of the boat and grinned.

"Now, boys," George the Bear continued. "Two beavers are using this beaver house right now."

"Are they sleeping inside now?" I asked.

"Probably. I see them just about every evening when I'm out here fishing around sundown."

"Show us where your lucky fishing spot is," I begged.

"Well, now, you've got to know that's a secret," George the Bear replied. "But I'll show you boys kind of where it is."

With that he restarted the outboard, slowly turned the boat out toward the main part of the lake, and kept us going for several minutes before shutting down again.

"All right now," he said. "My lucky fishing spot is somewhere between the beaver house and here."

"That's all you're going to tell us?" I asked.

"Yes, sir. That's all I'm going to tell you." Then he smiled and we were off once more heading to our favorite picnic site at the far end of the lake.

There is a large sandstone cliff at one end of Hungry Jack Lake. My family has always called this the Palisade though the Forest Service has labeled it Honeymoon Bluff. Below this cliff and to the left as you face it is a small point with a bit of a treeless rise at its center covered in crushed sandstone. This is the spot we called Old Baldy. In my boyhood days, summer would just not be complete without a picnic here with George the Bear.

My brothers and I became little troopers once George the Bear secured the boat to a tree. Following his directives, we formed a chain gang and unloaded all the goodies Mom supplied, taking extra caution with the pop bottles and the Thermos of coffee. We spread everything out on a level spot up top of Old Baldy. We laughed, gorged on lunch, told silly riddles, and threw rocks in the lake. George the Bear then sat on a log and lit his pipe. He was amazingly patient and indulging with the three of us. His smile was genuine, and it was clear he was enjoying himself immensely.

I remember thinking maybe this would be the day he would give one of us an empty Prince Albert tobacco tin. We coveted these little red cans. They were perfect for storing the tiny treasures of boyhood: agates, coins, Tinker Toy parts and the like. They also made wonderful worm cans for bluegill fishing. Mostly, though, they were important to us because they came from him. Before his vacation was over, George the Bear made sure each of the three of us got a tin. In retrospect, I think he likely brought a few empties along with him from home. I do not imagine anyone went through quite that much pipe tobacco in two weeks. Besides, George the Bear had just that sort of kindness in him.

As our picnic drew to a close, there was still one last tradition. I quieted down in anticipation. We were all back in the boat and were on our way home to the lodge. George the Bear smiled at us and started singing "My Old Kentucky Home." Watching his face carefully and struggling to hear his voice over the whine of the outboard motor, I tried to catch every word and was filled with joy.

Sometimes George the Bear would drive us into Grand Marais as a special treat. My younger brothers and I were each given a whole dollar to spend however we wished at Joynes' Ben Franklin Store. Lunch typically was at the A&W, which was later torn down. It was on one such outing that I received an early lesson about the Land of in Between.

Back then any trip to town was a big deal when it did not include going to school or to church. Having George the Bear all to ourselves for the better part of a day was bliss. He must have had as much patience as we had energy. George the Bear was an Oldsmobile man. The summer Chris was five and I was six, he took the pair of us to town in his Oldsmobile Ninety-Eight. This sedan had a special dashboard feature called a Safety Spectrum Speedometer. Instead of a needle gage, a colored bar would run from left to right under a row of digits. Speeds up to thirty-five miles per hour were shown in green. The bar turned orange from thirty-five to sixty-five miles per hour and red beyond that. This feature fascinated Chris, who has always had a mind for the mechanical. He was eager to see that bar turn red, and on one long, straight stretch of the Gunflint Trail, George the Bear obliged. Chris was thoroughly delighted and grinned away like a little monkey.

I have never been particularly skilled with numbers, but at age six I did know what the speed limit was. It was one thing for Chris or for me to pretend to be racing down the Gunflint Trail in the old Model A truck. This was something entirely different. I just could not believe that George the Bear was speeding. He was our friend. He was a grown-up, and here he was speeding!

"You are not supposed to do this. You're a lawyer and you're breaking the law," I shouted. I was appalled. My eyes welled up with tears.

I have no idea whether George the Bear felt amused or chided by my outburst, but he immediately slowed the car. I grew quiet and stayed so for several miles. I was pondering: could a good man do a bad thing? Right was right and wrong was wrong. Wasn't that the way it was supposed to work? How could there be something in the middle?

Chris was the one who pulled me away from my pondering. We had a bond and a ritual. It automatically went into action at a particular point on the Gunflint Trail where we both knew exactly how much farther it was to town. Upon reaching that spot, we would always turn to each other, smile and sing out, "Right around the corner is the lumber yard."

A hamburger and a frosty mug of root beer worked wonders to restore my faith in George the Bear. In Joynes' he put his big hand on my shoulder and said he never meant to upset me. Then he smiled down at me and said, "How about helping me pick out something to bring home for Tad?"

Together we decided that a terry cloth tee shirt with a picture of a deer on the front would be just right for the youngest McDonnell. Chris piped up that the cloth reminded him of what always hung from the towel rack at home.

"He'll be Taddy Washrag Shirt," he said.

Sure enough, that was one name with staying power. The three of us climbed into the front seat of the Oldsmobile and headed back to Gateway Lodge well within the speed limit. I had no words for it at the time, but I was beginning to figure out that a person is far more than the sum of his actions. That this lesson came from one I loved and admired made it all the richer.

Were I to plumb the depths of my memory, I would surely find signs of love and influence from Mom's father and stepmother. Dad's father died long before my parents were married. Grandmother McDonnell only once traveled to Gateway. Though we were assured of our grandparents' love, an appreciation for where we lived was something they sorely lacked. Mom's father, our Grandpa Charlie, simply could not grasp the concept of a preserved forest. What was the use of land that one could not plow or trees that would never be harvested? By contrast, George the Bear fully loved these woods and these waters. He was never shy about letting us know how much Gateway and the McDonnell family meant to him.

The summer of 1966 started out great. George the Bear had done a terrific job of keeping in touch over the previous winter. He sent us a Christmas package, and he booked his vacation well in advance of his June arrival. He even crated up his beloved Johnson outboard motor and shipped it to us long before the ice was off Hungry Jack Lake. We stored it in the pump house until he was ready for it, and we looked forward to his two weeks at Gateway every bit as much as he did.

George the Bear always got a lot of rest the first couple of days of his vacation. Mom told us he was hibernating and made it clear that we were not to disturb him. His law practice in Owensboro and his duties as an officer of the Kentucky Bar Association kept him plenty busy. This solo trip was to be restorative; his chance to fish, relax, and catch up on his sleep.

It was unlike the man to ever complain. When he came into the lodge office and quietly told my parents that he was experiencing severe chest pains, Dad immediately drove him to the hospital in Grand Marais. Somehow I knew this was not going to end well. Several of the lodge guests began asking about the kind fellow who was no longer in the dining room at meal times. When they began speaking of him in the past tense, I cleared out with tears in my eyes unable to handle what I was hearing. George the Bear's big heart gave out and he died the next day.

Mom rarely took time off from her work in the lodge kitchen, but meeting with Virginia Wilson when she arrived at her husband's deathbed was something she just had to do. Mom wanted to try to console Virginia, and she made certain she got to town to do so. When she got back home to the lodge, she called all of us kids into the staff dining room and told us the particulars of George the Bear's passing. Mom had a tough time getting the words out, and I had a tough time taking them in. Here I was grieving and hurting far more than I ever had at Grandmother McDonnell's passing in Chicago the previous summer. I felt confused and more than a little guilty about my grief. Guilt can be merciless at such times. Such are the workings of a little boy's mind and heart.

In an old box filled with family keepsakes and snapshots that Mom has collected over the years, there is one large photograph of George the Bear. He is seated at his spot in the dining room at Gateway Lodge wearing his tan jacket. He is lighting his pipe. There is, of course, a red pocket tin of Prince Albert tobacco on the table in front of him. The expression on his face is the very definition of a contented man. And yes, of course, he most certainly is family.

Becoming Locals

ateway Lodge was in every sense of the term a family business. It was our home as well as our livelihood. The lodge as we knew it was always a seasonal venture, and that season went pretty much full blast from ice out to just beyond the first hard frost. We made the lodge a success by our putting to use the same tools that help make a family succeed. These are cooperation, creativity, patience, compromise, and at times sacrifice. In truth, it took a bit of trial and error to hammer out all of the major lodge logistics. In time, both the buzz of the summer rush and the peace of the off-season developed their own predictable patterns.

Though Mom and Dad could be insanely busy during the height of the summer, the blessing for us kids was that they were usually accessible and never far away. They had the simplest of commutes to work each morning. My parents earned the majority of their income from early May to early October rarely taking a day for themselves in the duration. They always breathed easier in mid-autumn by which time the guests had all gone home. Our patience was then well rewarded, and we celebrated the end of each summer rush with a family cookout supper down on the shore of Hungry Jack Lake.

Mom and Dad had originally intended that Gateway Lodge would become our permanent year-round address beginning with our first summer season. However, both weather and circumstance conspired against this plan. My parents' fifth child was ready to be born in late autumn of 1958, but the hospital in Grand Marais was still under construction and was not yet ready for stork deliveries. Mom's sister and brother-in-law graciously offered to share with us their home in Grand Forks, North Dakota until the next McDonnell showed up and was fit to travel. My brother, Tad, arrived on the 26th of November just as a horrific storm was pounding Grand Marais and the entire north shore of Lake Superior.

The storm was a killer, paralyzing much of the Upper Midwest. While Grand Marais was getting clobbered, Grand Forks experienced its own unique blizzard blend of snow and wind-blown topsoil known locally as a snirt storm. Chicago winters were never quite like this. Heeding advice from relatives to stay put and to hunker down, Mom and Dad found us a suitable Grand Forks apartment for the winter. They enrolled Jack and Kath in a nearby elementary school, postponing progress on the myriad lodge projects until the arrival of spring.

At the close of our family's second summer at Gateway Lodge, Mom and Dad moved us all down the Gunflint Trail and took over management of Seawall Motel in Grand Marais while the owners wintered in Florida. In what little free time they had, they also helped to manage the local ski hill. That Christmas my family was able to reciprocate for the generosity of our North Dakota kin by hosting a large family reunion. There is nothing quite like having an entire motel available for such an event. When the snows at last abated, we took to the woods once more. Mom once again put the lodge kitchen in order ramping up for the summer blitz, and Dad once again led the efforts to modernize the next couple of cabins on the docket.

During the school year of 1960-1961, Mom and Dad took over the management of Mable's Café in Grand Marais while Mable herself headed south to stay warm. We rented the bottom floor of a large duplex in town, and Jack and Kath were able to walk to school. My parents worked hard to transfer to this setting the fine reputation for good food and warm hospitality they had earned with their efforts at Gateway Lodge. This was all wasted on one logger, however, who ordered a bowl of stew at the café one evening. He bellowed his angry complaint that my mother had placed a birch leaf in his supper. This bellicose fellow may have been an ace with axe and chainsaw, but he was pitifully ignorant with regard to food seasonings unable to differentiate a birch leaf from a bay leaf. Of course, having to placate the occasional clueless customer has always been a part of what it means to be in my parents' line of work. Mom and Dad went the extra mile to make the locals happy, and by so doing they made a positive name for themselves.

By the time I was to start kindergarten, my parents decided we would no longer winter away from the woods, babysitting another person's business for the winter months. Mom and Dad succeeded in lobbying the county for school bus service on the Gunflint Trail. The kicker in all of this was that Dad became the school bus driver. As the captain of his giant orange craft, Dad stocked up on cases of ether starting fluid, carburetor cleaner, and Heet, an alcohol-based product designed to keep engine fuel lines ice-free. He brought the school bus battery indoors on most winter nights to keep it from freezing and to hook it up to his newly acquired battery charger. Of necessity, he became a master hand with jumper cables and a fierce battler of the tire chain demons.

Ever a creature of habit, Dad had a set routine he followed religiously as road conditions permitted. He kept a car in town so that he could head back to the lodge after the morning run. This meant a lot of time behind the wheel, but it also permitted him to put in a few hours of work and to have lunch with Mom and the youngest McDonnell boys. He would then head back to town and arrive just before school let out in the afternoon. Dad was as reliable as they come, and he took all of his duties to heart. He was a good driver. Before long the tan twill cap he often wore had a couple blue-and-gold safe-operator award pins attached to it.

It made sense for Dad to become the Gunflint Trail school bus driver, as several of the riders for the run from Gateway Lodge into town were his own progeny. My siblings and I were never all that thrilled about having to rise in the dark most winter mornings, but there was a blessing of sorts in our being among the very first families notified of snow-related school cancelations. After a hot breakfast, those of us of school age bundled up and tromped out to board the bus. Dad always started the bus and kept it running during breakfast in order to warm up the engine. He usually remembered to unplug the headbolt heater before we took off, but the many patches of electrician's tape wrapped around the long extension cord running from the house to the driveway gave testimony to memory lapses.

Our first stop was Trail Center, where Dad would turn the bus around and wait for Mr. Dailey to show up driving the little orange van we called the Cheese Box. The two Dailey sisters and any other students from the upper region of the Gunflint Trail would then transfer from the Cheese Box to Dad's bus. Being a small McDonnell kid aboard this bus had its privileges. I often sat on the boxed heater just to the left of the driver's seat and helped Dad by working the lever that controlled the stop sign as other kids boarded or got off the bus. Yes, these were less litigious times. Perhaps we were all the better for that.

I also remember having to sit on the top step of the school bus as my time-out punishment when I quarreled with my siblings. This was never fun. The road was long and bumpy. Dad was not a particularly strict disciplinarian, but he was consistent. All of the McDonnell kids riding that bus spent a bit of sit-and-think time on that blasted top step.

With school transportation logistics finally well in hand, my parents turned their attention to winterizing our cabin home. This entailed replacing the front porch with an enclosure that gave us more bedroom space. The addition of an insulated vestibule, also known as an arctic entryway, provided us with a mudroom and a bit more storage. A new gas floor furnace replaced the cabin's ancient oil heater. The grid of this furnace was set right into the floorboards, and this became the most coveted spot for changing out of jammies and into school duds. Mom tried her hand at masonry and found it much to her liking. She fashioned a fine brick base and back piece for our new Franklin stove. Dad kept us well supplied with firewood.

Frozen plumbing, spit baths, the piddle pot, and trips to Grand Marais on laundry days became routine parts of our winter life together. So, too, did the seasonal window coverings made from semi-opaque plastic sheeting stretched out on wooden frames, which served as our storm windows. These were an inexpensive and efficient means of keeping the heat in and the winds out, but the effect was akin to living for months at a time inside a giant waxed paper sandwich wrapper. Mom absolutely hated these. We all knew that spring was right around the corner when she wrote in bold letters at the top of the to do list: REMOVE WINDOW PLASTICS . . . HALLELUIAH!

It was not unusual for the power to go out during winter storms, and we had several kerosene lamps and a large box of candle stubs for just such an occurrence. The candles were leftovers from those used in the lodge dining room during the summer. Having them lit around our home during one particular power outage gave Mom an idea that gradually involved all of us kids. She had already figured out one way to generate a bit of winter income and was busy designing gift baskets to sell via mail order to former lodge guests. This allowed people to get a little taste of the north woods while reminding them of summer at Gateway Lodge. One of the prized possessions of any Gunflint Trail resort owner or canoe outfitter is his or her carefully maintained client mailing list. Using the Gateway list, Mom sent out flyers advertising her baskets. She then stocked up on about a gazillion mailing boxes. Mom bought the baskets themselves from a wholesaler, placed two or three of jars of her homemade berry jams in each, and decorated each with a bit of greenery from the woods around Hungry Jack. It was up to us kids to collect berries in the summer and greenery any time it was needed. The baskets were a hit, and before long Mom decided to also offer gift candles.

Soon we were making Christmas candles by melting stubs in an old coffee can on the stove and raiding our school supplies for a few choice broken crayons to melt into the mix for color. Mom favored a pale green. Setting wicking into place, we poured liquid wax into two tea cups, inverted the cups when the wax had hardened, and joined the two pieces to make a single round ball. Mom figured out a way to make what looked just like white frosting out of paraffin wax whipped with the beaters of her electric mixer. When the candles were frosted and set on a sprig of cedar greenery, the effect was both festive and charming. These became popular gift items. Since the frosting was spread in much the same manner used to construct a sandwich, we took to calling these round candles peanut butter bombs.

As comforting as candles are once the power goes out, they do little to help cope with frozen pipes. Like most Gunflint Trail residents, we drew our water from the nearest lake and had our own chlorinator unit. Grey water discharge and effluents were handled by a septic tank system that required frequent monitoring and maintenance. Dad, who never once had to consider the functions of basic utilities prior to moving to the woods, spent many winter hours wrestling with the consequences of our far-from-reliable plumbing. By chatting with a few long-time locals, he made a valiant attempt to acquire all the information he could about keeping our waterlines from freezing.

Information, though, is different from wisdom. It is a sad truth that some skills can only be obtained with the doing. Had we a deep well, a foolproof power source, or a thirty-two-mile pipe to the public water system in Grand Marais, my dear father's Gateway Lodge winters would have passed far more peaceably. Dad possessed more of an academic bend than any flare for the practical. His degree in philosophy from the University of Notre Dame counted for squat each time he ended up chopping a hole in the ice at the end of the boat dock to get drinking water for the family. What he was obtaining through his efforts was a doctorate in frustration at the school of hard knocks.

To keep things flowing as they should in the winter, the basic tenet for home owners about never mixing water and electricity has to be fudged a bit in order to correctly install heat trace cable units for water and septic lines. It is also essential to understand when not to flush and when not to use antifreeze. It took some time for Dad to get this all down pat and to realize that much of our less-than-dependable plumbing system had been improperly cobbled together in the first place. That being said, we were never without water with which to drink, to cook, or to wash no matter how many trips to the hole in the ice it required.

Dad was a bit clumsy at times, as was evidenced one midwinter morning when he tripped on the threshold and spilled the piddle pot. The air was blue for quite some time with words never intended for small ears. I am most assuredly my father's boy, for that same threshold snagged my foot one spring morning causing me to trip and break a jar of molasses all over the floor and all over myself.

Home for most of Dad's growing up years had been a well-appointed Chicago apartment where the building supervisor was summoned for any and all maintenance needs. Winter at Gateway Lodge was an entirely different universe for him. In retrospect, I have come to admire Dad's stubborn persistence, for he learned most of what he ever was to know about wintering in the woods and becoming a local there through what must have been for him the most humbling means possible.

Schooling, Fooling, and Retooling

f all the values I learned as a child, few have served as consistently as love of place. The forest was both my home and my playground. It was where I retreated physically whenever I could, and retreating to the forest mentally became my default mode whenever my self-confidence took a header. In my earliest school years, I was unsettled as a student and probably more than a little unsettling for certain of my teachers. I was a daydreamer, often preoccupied with my own happy imaginings and seldom entirely certain what to take seriously. The tiny switch in my brain that toggled from play to work was often stuck on the setting that was all wrong for the particular instructional activity of the moment. The more I struggled as a learner, the more my attention wandered off to the woods.

In kindergarten, I quickly became a master hand at playtime. Two of my fellow five-year-olds, Danny and Rick, could well attest to this. They used to dump all the blocks out of the block cart, put me in it, and push me around the wooden floors of the kindergarten room until we either crashed spectacularly or I became too loud in my glee. Usually both happened, and Mrs. Tollifson, our teacher, would put the brakes on our hotrodding.

When it came time to shift from play to instruction in basic phonics, my mind drifted. I found the classroom ant farm particularly captivating. How did all those ants get in there anyway? What did they grow on their farm? Did they have ant hoedowns on Saturday nights? What if they all wore tiny farmer overalls, carried tiny pitchforks, and drove around on tiny tractors? That would be great. Nope, Mrs. Tollifson's phonics and pre-reading instruction just did not register with this boy.

Mrs. Tollifson advised my parents to strongly consider holding me back for a second year of kindergarten. In this she was fully justified. I had a late summer birthday, was struggling in school to capture basic concepts, and was far smaller than the majority of my classmates. However, Mom and Dad decided to keep me on the same track as my classmates figuring I would eventually catch up with them. After all, the first two McDonnell children were thriving as students. Timmy would come around in his own good time.

I headed off to Mrs. Jackson's first grade classroom wretchedly disappointed to discover that the ant farm stayed behind. There was no block cart. What was this anyway? My classmates gave me a bit of ribbing for having the same name as Sally's stuffed bear in the Dick and Jane readers we used in class, but that was fine. What I was beginning to find bothersome was how quickly my buddies were moving ahead to thicker, longer readers while I stayed with the little kid starter books. Do not let anyone tell you that a six-year-old never notices such a thing.

I became considerably self-conscious as a student and hated reading aloud in school. Mom would sit down with me at home to help me practice. She was patient, consistently supportive, and had some experience as a successful tutor. During the two years we wintered in Grand Marais, Mom home schooled Jack and Kath for a few weeks in the autumn, while the lodge was still open, and again in the spring, when we were back in the woods ramping up for another Gateway tourist season. At the suggestion of other Gunflint Trail families and with the full blessing of the local school district, Mom secured materials from the Calvert Home School Curriculum and turned the staff dining room into a classroom for Jack and Kath. She made certain they kept up with their lessons. I remember being told never to interrupt while Mom was conducting class. I also remember covering the blackboard she used with chalk curlicues when she was finished one afternoon and asking her if my marks looked anything like real writing. She nodded and smiled. Then I baffled her by insisting she read it and tell me what it said. My being both stubborn and quite clueless as to alphabet fundamentals might have given her some insight to my future as a learner.

It required a great deal of patience to sit down with me and try to help me learn to read, for I was glacially slow at decoding. I felt defeated, and that brought out the whiner in me. Short vowel sounds were my nemesis. I could seldom distinguish one from another. When I was a second grader, a couple of volunteer moms came to school to conduct hearing tests. I thought the audiometer they brought in with them looked pretty cool with those big dials. Clamping a set of earphones on my head was all it took to make me imagine I was a jet pilot. When it came to responding to the beeps and warbles, some were easy to detect. Some I was unsure about, so I put my hand up as many times as I figured the kid ahead of me had. Somehow I passed this testing. No one at home suspected that I had any trouble hearing. It would be more than ten years before I had any additional audiological evaluation.

My teachers tagged me as a fairly bright child with a hesitancy to apply myself to the rigors of learning. This hesitancy became part of a self-perpetuating cycle, for the less success I experienced, the less willing I was to put effort into something with which I struggled. When I opened the envelope containing my report card on my final day of third grade, I read that I had passed on trial and was not at all certain what that meant. Being the type of reader I was, I thought my teacher had written that I had passed on trail, as in Gunflint Trail. Though the wording did seem a bit odd, I felt gratified and a bit proud of her acknowledgement that my family had its home not in town but up in the lake country. Mom and Dad later clued me into the gravity of my status.

That summer I worried about what life would be like in grade four. Distraction from my uneasiness came in late June, as Chris and I began to prepare for first communion and first reconciliation at Saint John's Catholic Church in Grand Marais. Nuns came in from Duluth to serve as our instructors, and they were the first teachers I ever experienced who were also members of a religious order. Dad made certain we got into town each day for classes and was there at our celebratory Mass. I remember being completely in awe of these sisters and of the idea of giving one's life totally to the church. Latin and the Mass were so mysterious. I fully doubted that I would ever have the makings of a suitable priest. However, I found the blending of spirituality with instruction entirely to my liking.

Meanwhile, Dad was taking bets on how short-lived this newly found state of grace would be for his two rambunctious boys.

I had the rare distinction of getting the same teacher in fourth grade that I had in kindergarten. Mrs. Tollifson's classroom was down in the basement of the antiquated stack of bricks that was Cook County Elementary. Its dungeon-like setting seemed all too fitting. I had a strong sense that the school year was going to be hellish from the start when some of the guys played hallway kickball with my brand new lunchbox, ruining its lid on the third day of classes. My initial suspicions could not have been more correct. By that time, I was aware that Mrs. Tollifson had wanted me to repeat kindergarten. I figured now that she again had me in her clutches, she would be out for blood.

To her credit, Mrs. Tollifson signed me up right away for remedial reading lessons with Mrs. Ann Clark, the school's reading specialist. That went pretty well, and I recall having a great rapport with Mrs. Clark. She and her husband, Dave, had strong roots on the Gunflint Trail. They had owned and operated Rockwood Lodge in the late 1940s. Rockwood Lodge still exists. It is on Poplar Lake just a few miles up the trail from the turnoff to the Hungry Jack Lake Road. Dave Clark had earned a reputation as a keen hunter, an excellent fishing guide, and a peerless man of the woods. The Clarks owned the duplex my family rented in Grand Marais the winter Mom and Dad operated Mable's Café.

Once I made the connection between Mrs. Clark and the Gunflint Trail, she could do no wrong in my eyes. I wanted to stay in her remedial reading room full time where I felt successful and appreciated, where I was finally beginning to read and enjoy chapter books, and where I was not seen as being slow or stupid. That, of course, could not happen. The chasm between my development as a learner and that of my fourth-grade classmates was growing ever wider, and I was miserable. This time, when Mom and Dad conferenced with Mrs. Tollifson and she outlined her recommendation for my retention, they acquiesced. They also decided to retain Chris, who had struggles of his own. Chris was finishing up his school year with the same third-grade teacher who had taught me. At the year-end conference with Mom, this teacher shared of Chris: "He don't do so good in language." Small wonder.

Chris seemed unfazed when Mom outlined the decisions she, Dad, and the school made regarding our retentions. I, on the other hand, was devastated. All the careful words and all the supportive comments backed up with love that Mom put into her explanation never hit home with anything near the power of the images that flashed through my brain of my former classmates, who would be calling me Dummy or Flunker on the playground in September. Chris told me decades later that he had only experienced one or two days during all of his schooling that he fully enjoyed. These were field trip days. The rest of it he just did not care about in the slightest. While Chris took Mom's message pretty much in stride, I trembled, imagining Mrs. Tollifson with her feet up on her desk and her arms folded, laughing maniacally.

Today, when I reflect on what it took Chris to reach the high level of success he presently enjoys, I am filled with admiration for his tenacity and his self-confident manner. He took the common belief that one cannot go far without a solid education and turned it right on its ear. Though Chris holds no affection whatsoever for teachers that put him through school days he would just as soon forget, he has never begrudged me for my becoming an educator. He and I were once like twins. Our paths began to diverge greatly the autumn we were both held back.

My second dose of fourth grade did a world of good to help me settle down and concentrate on my schoolwork. I credit this positive change to my new teacher, Mrs. Creighton, who collaborated with my parents to make certain I knew her high expectations. Mrs. Creighton effectively cured me of inattentiveness during her verbal instruction by demanding that I maintain consistent eye contact and actively participate in all class discussions. She made certain all the students in her charge understood that education was not a spectator sport. Because of her commitment, her caring, and her high quality of instruction, I was gradually able to find a fair measure of success as a student.

Socially, however, I was a true mess. Unlike Chris, who kept most of his old friends and went on to make several more among his new classmates, I tended to isolate myself. Though I was teased but once, and this by a particularly nasty girl I was able to shut right up with a cruel but effective rejoinder, I had it in my head that my being retained meant that I was marked as shameful and of less value than my peers. I became apprehensive and cautious around anyone who was not family. Though I have always experienced an extremely low tolerance for noisy environments, I began to go well out of my way to seek quiet places both on the edges of the school playground and at home in the woods. When not in the classroom, I began retreating to my imagination more than ever before.

It would take years and much instruction from another fine group of nuns at a school a couple thousand miles away from the Gunflint Trail before I would earn respectable marks as a student. It would take even more years before I learned that my low threshold of tolerance for loud environments actually had an organic cause and stemmed from sensorineural hearing loss and a condition I experience known as auditory recruitment. To help compensate for malfunctioning nerve endings in the cochlea, the brain of a person with this condition tries to "recruit" healthy nerve endings to fill in the gaps. This often results in distorted signals reaching the brain perceived as being much louder than they were ever intended. When an individual's hearing is malfunctioning and loud noises are perceived with heightened intensity, that individual naturally seeks balance. I gradually discovered that symmetry was something I could most readily find in the quiet of the wilderness.

What others had misinterpreted as a willful lack of attention was in reality one ramification of a moderate-to-severe bilateral hearing loss. Though I most likely was born with this condition, it was not fully diagnosed until I was in college and was struggling to understand the voices of my pupils during my student teaching practicum. I suspect most adults have a few aspects of their upbringing that would cause them to reflect: If I only knew then what I know now. This is one of mine. However, instead of treading water in a pool of regret, I choose to push forward pausing on occasion to give the very best of my upbringing a fond and lingering backward glance.

The forest works well for me as my fail-safe because I come to it with all of my senses, not just my broken hearing. I have faith in my ability to find there and garner the peace I seek. This is faith born of consistency of experience. As a boy, I made no clear distinction between Saint John's Catholic Church and the woods around Gateway Lodge as sacred ground where God resides. This is why preservation of wilderness is so ingrained in who I am. To trash a part of a forest is to desecrate an altar. As an adult, I try with some success to put into practice what the nuns struggled to teach me so many years ago; each of us is a dwelling place for the Creator. That being the case, we had better not trash each other.

Caution: Boy at Work

O n every summer day except Sundays and the Fourth of July, the mail would arrive at Gateway Lodge sometime between eleven o'clock in the morning and lunchtime. One of the summer homeowners would usually gather it up in a large bundle and bring it in from the mailboxes out on the Gunflint Trail. The post office did not offer door-to-door delivery where we lived, and the lodge was the gathering spot for most folks on our side of the lake. If our friends Ginny and Neil Selvig brought in the mail bundle, my siblings and I knew they were up at their summer cabin and would be driving at least some of us to town for Mass on Sunday. This was a kindness the Selvigs often did for my parents, who were busy attending to the needs of the resort guests. If Willis Salisbury was the fellow who brought in the mail bundle, Chris and I would smile at each other and wait for Dad's inevitable comment: "You know, boys, that clown drives like a bat out of hell."

When we were quite young, Chris and I were often given the responsibility of sorting letters and newspapers and delivering the mail to nearby summer homeowners. Mom and Dad were usually fully aware of who was up on the lake and who was not and would clue us in. Chris and I had a bit of a sly racket going with this delivery job. We knew full well that Ann Hanover and Ellen Zimmerman were both pushovers and would give us candy. We were shameless moochers. Little brother Tad was small and cute, and we soon discovered we took in a far better haul when we brought him along with us. Of course, Mom frowned upon treats immediately before lunch. We figured that what Mom didn't know wouldn't hurt us one bit. The clang of the meal bell let us know when it was time to hurry back to the lodge, and we would laugh and chase each other home chewing on caramels the entire way.

As the lodge telephone was one of only a few on the lake in those days, taking telephone messages was a common chore. Sometimes it was my job to deliver these messages. Down the lake a bit was a summer home owned by the Minneapolis gangster and mob boss, Tommy Banks. I doubt that anyone fully knows the truth about Tommy Banks these days. However, three things are certain. First, as the leader of the Irish mob in the Twin Cities during and shortly after prohibition, he was greatly involved in vice activities. Second, Tommy Banks frequently traveled to his Hungry Jack Lake cabin and fished the area lakes in the company of armed bodyguards. Third, there is absolutely no truth to the assertion that his cabin home ever contained underground escape tunnels and elaborate hiding places. Anyone who has ever tried to dig a hole in this rocky country could tell you that.

Rumors and legends connected with Tommy Banks and his notorious past were plentiful when I was a kid. Stories and exaggerations put him right up there with Al Capone in my boyhood imagination. Bootlegger, gunrunner, racketeer, bank robber, jailbird, even suspected murderer; all of these were labels used to describe the man. All of these descriptors raced through my head the afternoon Dad sent me over to deliver a telephone message to Tommy Banks.

I can picture the seven-year-old version of myself knock-kneed and seriously concerned he might fill his shorts before completing his chore. I was scared and confused walking along the summer home road. Surely Dad had heard the rumors about Tommy Banks. Had my own father just given me a death sentence? Would I be kidnapped? This guy's name was Tommy. Did he have a Tommy gun? Would he use me for target practice? *Timmy the target, that's me. Maybe I should get a Timmy gun. Yeah, that would show him. Take that you dirty rat. . .A-A-A-A-A-A. I wish I had a get away car. Wait a minute. There's some old guy coming to the door. He looks like somebody's grandpa. No way! That can't be Tommy Banks. Where are all his goons and gun molls?*

The old gentleman could not have been kinder to me. He was appreciative of my efforts and was just as nice as any of the other summer homeowners. He even let me in to take a closer look at the large polar bear rug that hung from the wall of his living room. I had nothing to fear from the man. On my walk back to the lodge, I began to feel kind of sorry for Tommy Banks. I certainly was not the one to ask if a person wanted to know which labels and which rumors accurately fit the man. I remember thinking what a shame it was that this old man's past cut him off from other people living around the lake. The ugly rumors connected with him failed to do anyone any good.

In addition to delivering messages and showing guests around the lodge, I was occasionally given the task of helping to lug suitcases to and from the rental cabins. Sometimes the bags were larger than I was and outweighed me by a considerable margin. What I lacked in muscle I tried to make up for in enthusiasm. It was here that I learned the true value of always packing light for travel and the advisability of never giving too much teasing grief to any little fellow trying to help you upon arrival lest your bag be dropped in a mud puddle upon your departure.

MOM AND DAD WOULD SOMETIMES summon one or more of us kids and give us a more extensive guide duty to perform. This usually meant leading a hike up to Caribou Rock, a nearby scenic outcrop with a spectacular view down the length of West Bearskin Lake. These early experiences in helping people link up with their wilderness surroundings were often delightfully agreeable mixtures of work and play. Dad once tried to nurture an entrepreneurial spirit in Chris and me by suggesting that we expand our role as hike leaders and set up a lemonade stand at the Caribou Rock trailhead. Mostly in jest, he figured we could charge a dime a glass for those heading up the path and a quarter a glass for those thirstier hikers coming back down.

Although the idea of making a little pocket money was highly appealing and we pondered at great length the logistics of launching into business as pint-sized purveyors of liquid refreshment, it never got off the drawing board. Lemonade as we knew it was made from powdered lemon globules, which my parents bought by the case from the Sexton Food Company. As kids, we called the powder lemon globulosis, as if it were some yellowing skin disease akin to jaundice or leprosy. Instead of sugar, we always added what we called sweetness. That is, we used liquid Sucaryl, a sugar substitute. Older brother Jack had been diagnosed with type one diabetes before we moved from Chicago, and using sweetness was a concession my family always made for his sake. Sure, the final product could quench your thirst, but neither Chris nor I could actually picture selling the stuff. Chris and I also noticed that hikers invariably bought themselves cold soda pop as soon as they got back to the lodge. Mom and Dad would never have let us talk them into any deal where they bought all the pop and we sold it keeping all the profits; not that we didn't try.

Whenever we took guests up to Caribou Rock, most were plenty satisfied to reach the overlook, to spend a while taking photographs, to search for ripe blueberries, and to head back down to the lodge. However, when I was playing guide, I could sometimes talk a select few into extending their hike just a wee bit farther. This permitted us hikers to pass through a magnificent grove of old growth white pines and red pines on our way to the ridge overlooking Moss Lake. I loved standing beneath one of these old giant pines, listening to the sighing of the wind in the high branches, and inhaling the clean scent of the crystallized sap. It was from a similar grove of pines nearby on the shore of West Bearskin Lake that logs were harvested to build Gateway Lodge.

I was no more than eight years old and leading a husband and wife on a hike up to Caribou Rock and just that special wee bit farther when I learned all about pine knots. The three of us were looking out over Moss Lake and its unbroken shoreline. This couple seemed mighty impressed that there were no buildings, no roads, and not one single boat anywhere to be seen here. When the fellow pulled a gunnysack from the small pack he was carrying, I figured he was going to collect pinecones. That was before he began kicking at the underside of a rotted, moss-covered pine that had fallen decades before and was slowly feeding the soil from which it rose.

"What are you doing, looking for a bear's den?" I asked.

"Come over to this log and I'll show you," the fellow replied. "This is something you might want to know about since you like these old pines so much."

While his wife and I looked on, he reached down and pulled up a small, solid remnant of a branch from the decayed tree.

"Pine knot," he said. Then he tapped this piece of wood on a rock before handing it to me. "This will be the very last part of the tree to rot. Do you know why that is?"

"No," I said. "I'm not sure."

"Smell it."

When I put it to my face, there was a damp and somewhat musty smell. However, there was another scent that seemed to come from underneath the dampness, as if from the heart of the wood itself.

"Pine rosin," the fellow explained. "The pitch or the sap has collected where the branch once connected to the tree trunk. It keeps this part of the tree from rotting away as quickly as the trunk will. Do you want to help us collect a few of these?"

"Sure," I answered, "but what are you going to do with them?"

"We dry them out at home for a while," he replied. "Then, when we have a nice bed of coals going in the fireplace, we set a pine knot on the top. It will burn for a long while."

"It gives a wonderful glow," the lady shared, "and it always reminds us of a day spent in the forest."

"There are just a couple of ground rules here," the fellow said. "Try to take a knot from the underside of the log if you can, and please do cover up any scar you make with moss. Any other people coming by here should not have to see a mess."

The three of us had the gunnysack filled before long. On our way back down the trail, we paused beneath one giant white pine and watched as the wind tossed the topmost branches.

"That wind is the very breath of God Himself," the lady said.

Her sentiment was unlike anything I had ever heard in my catechism classes, and I decided I liked it. If this forest was where I felt happiest and if I was made in God's image, then it made perfect sense that God would be happy here, too.

When we got back to the lodge, this gracious couple gave me half of the pine knots and thanked me for spending the afternoon with them. They both earnestly shook my hand, and I will tell you that can mean quite a lot to an eight-year-old boy trying his hardest to appear older than the sum of his years. I set my collection of pine knots on the roof of the woodshed behind the lodge and let them dry in the sun for several weeks. When summer was almost over and the dining room grew less crowded each evening, I sparingly doled out my dried pine knots occasionally adding one to the evening fire. The fire would then glow with spits and spurts of yellow, orange, and blue as the rosin deposits ignited. It was as if the dried wood were alive once again. Perhaps in this action I was in some way setting free the spirit of the old pine.

LOOKING BACK UPON MY FAMILY'S Gateway years from my present perspective, I am unable to delineate one abrupt, seminal moment when I shifted from a child at play to a steady part of the lodge's work crew. That process was gradual. Well before either of us was in our teens, Chris and I were often given tasks such as raking leaves from the cabin paths, hauling brush to the burn pile down by the old ice house, smoothing out the beach sand after a big rain, or spreading gravel to fill in the puddles in the parking lot. Mom and Dad did not ride herd on us and seldom checked in on our progress. As often as not, we had temporarily checked out and suspended brush hauling to build a fort from dead tree branches. Rakes were set aside as we buried each other in leaf piles. The beach would become even more torn up while we built miniature towns in the sand complete with their own rivers, hills, and roadways. Small boys are, of course, magnetically and hopelessly attracted to puddles with the all too predictable consequences. Though little progress was visible, my parents' key objectives were well met. We were out of their hair and pleasantly occupied.

As a child, my Saturday evening job was to stay out of the kitchen, to stay out of trouble, and to make certain my younger brothers did likewise. Summer Saturdays were the busiest times of all at Gateway, for Saturday night was Chuck Wagon Night. Mom and Dad set out a huge all-you-can-eat buffet and opened the dining room to all comers. This became immensely popular with the lodge guests, with area summer homeowners, and with several townies, who traveled up the Gunflint Trail for a pleasant evening. Jack's first steady employment at the lodge was running the dishwasher on Saturday nights. This was a gigantic double tub beast set into a sheet metal counter. When I was deemed large enough to run the dishwasher with minimal risk of falling into one of the tubs, I gradually replaced Jack. He seemed quite pleased to have me take over his role as Gateway's man about suds. Mom gave me an apron and my very own pair of rubber gloves. I enjoyed being part of the action.

My job was to scrape the plates, empty the glasses, and load and transfer the dish racks from tub to tub. Scalding wash and rinse water meant a fellow had to be careful. The crowd of hungry diners meant a fellow had to be quick. Pay off came in the late evening when I got to go through the buffet line myself. Set me up with a plate of roast beef, a couple of Mom's deviled eggs, a large slice of her German chocolate cake with a cream puff on the side for good measure, and I would willingly wash dishes until the loons came home.

My summers at Gateway planted the seeds of a strong service mentality. For me, this became the flipside of a solidly established play imperative. My work ethic and my play ethic were both nurtured by the examples Mom and Dad set down for my siblings and for me. My parents worked diligently to ensure the lodge guests were enjoying themselves. For the most part, Mom and Dad took great pleasure in doing so and were never shy about expressing that pleasure. Dad was never more animated than when putting together a daylong fishing trip to Saganaga Lake or Northern Light Lake, the big border waters near the end of the Gunflint Trail. He and his party of guests would come back to the lodge in the late evening all smiles and laden with heavy stringers of monstrous pike. I so wanted to be one of those guys along with him.

Mom added to the joy of those evenings with her teasing about the party coming in far too late to expect any supper. She would then set out an excellent feed for them, take full delight in their gratitude, and show few signs of being bone weary. In time each of us kids mastered a unique sense of commitment to task and to the people we served. This was balanced with a keen awareness of the importance of simply goofing off when the need strikes.

Hired Help

O ne might easily construe that a resort-owning couple with six children is blessed with a built-in work crew. There is plenty of truth in that assumption, but make no mistake. Nothing was automatic. That crew's ability to function effectively did not just happen all on its own. My siblings and I had to grow into the various opportunities life at the lodge presented. The several men and women, who shared summers at Gateway with us as the hired help, impacted that growth substantially.

From the very beginning, Mom and Dad hired a handyman each summer. This continued until Jack learned to drive and to pound nails and was fully able to assume the role of handyman on his own. While most of these fellows were good-tempered, suitably skilled at carpentry, and kid-tolerant, my family's first Gateway Lodge handyman was, to quote my mother, "a real piece of work." We inherited this gem from the Gapen family, and I will refer to him as Frank lest his ornery ghost stir malevolently with my disparaging references.

I cannot clearly picture Frank in the context of that first Gateway summer, as I was not quite three years old. However, I did meet the man when he dropped by the lodge in his later years. Mom recalls vividly a certain deficiency in personal hygiene that was this fellow's trademark. On one occasion in the staff dining room, she was at a loss to determine who emitted the more offensive aroma. Was it Chris with his full and sagging diaper, or was it Frank with his lack of affinity for hot water and a bar of soap?

Frank earned my parents' eternal wrath one morning by grumbling quite audibly when asked to clear out all the brush along the cabin paths and around the rental cabins themselves. His reply: "Damn city people. They're gonna turn this whole place into a Chicago nigger park." That was not exactly an endearing sentiment. Frank was not rehired the following summer. I suspect his unannounced visit years later derived from curiosity to learn firsthand just how dismally that young Chicago couple with all those kids had failed in their efforts. If this was his aim, I am happy to report that he left unsatisfied. Frank rolled in driving an older model pickup with a camper shell. He looked around a bit, spoke briefly with Mom, and departed never to darken our door again.

I can recall clearly and with fondness an older couple from the Duluth/Superior Twin Ports area, who worked for us the summer I turned six. Joe and Ardis went together like two worn shoes. Ardis was lean, all smiles, and full of energy. She seemed always to have a kind word for the pesky little boys frequently underfoot. Her counterpart, Joe, moved slowly and as if in a world of pain known only to himself. He was built quite a bit lower to the ground than his wife, and he walked as if a long life of miserable toil had started to push him into the earth. Joe was not exactly what you would call a self-starter. He could grump a bit when it suited him to do so, but it was pretty easy for my brothers and me to get him to laugh.

When I picture Ardis, I see her in my mind's eye busy ironing, cleaning cabins, or doing the laundry. She was the consummate model of cheerful industry. When I picture Joe, he walks about the lodge grounds at a glacial pace in his old blue overalls. Just above his right back pocket are the yellow remains of the deviled egg Chris threw at him, and it is going on two weeks since Chris hit him square in the butt. Rather than cream my little brother for being bratty, Joe elected to wear the evidence of his being wronged by a four-year-old with a pretty good arm. Then again, perhaps Joe actually did sleep in those overalls, never removing them, as my siblings and I always suspected.

Joe would usually let Chris and me ride shotgun in the truck when it came time to do a dump run. A resort serving three full meals each day to its guests generates a lot of garbage, which in turn attracts a lot of bears. Frequent trips to the area landfill helped to keep the bears away from the lodge. Joe often threatened to throw my brother and me to the biggest bear on the garbage heap, but we knew he was all bluff. We also knew this group of black bears was nothing more than a bunch of mooching cowards looking for an easy feed. We learned from experience that they were easy to scare off when they came too close to the truck's tailgate to sniff the odd bag of fish guts. Little boys were simply not on their menu.

On one particular dump run, the three of us had just passed Leo Lake. Joe downshifted and we began climbing the long hill near the gravel pit. Red pines bordered the road on both sides. The grove on one side was clearly posted as private property. All of a sudden Joe slammed on the brakes. My brother and I stared at him in wonder.

"What's wrong?" we asked in tandem.

"Didn't you little rug rats see that sign?" he replied.

"Yeah. So what?"

"Well boys," said Joe. We're in the middle of a forest and that sign says NO TREE PASSING. If we go any farther, we'll be breaking the law. The cops will throw us all in jail for sure. Now I wouldn't mind seeing you two little skunks behind bars, but me and Ardis got plans for the evening."

Chris and I looked at each other. Then we both looked over at Joe, as if he had just announced we were all on our way to Mars. Joe took in the seriousness of our expressions and burst out laughing. That night I chuckled as I said my bedtime prayers asking God to forgive us our tree passing as we forgive those who tree pass against us. In retrospect, it is a marvel that Chris and I ever became literate.

WHEN I REFLECT ON THE MINIATURE version of me, who was running around the resort trying not to be too much of a pest, I feel gratitude for a few indelible impressions left by certain of our hired help. I have always been drawn to intelligent women. In truth, it is not in my nature to pay the slightest bit of attention to any other kind. All of this started early. The wait staff for the dining room at Gateway consisted of two or three college girls, who signed on for the summer in order to earn money to help finance another year of their education.

In rotating shifts, these girls changed into the green-and-white uniforms Mom sewed for them and took care of the lodge guests. When the shifts were over, they donned their regular clothes to clean cabins, to take care of the laundry, or to handle any of the hundreds of other tasks that made up a typical day keeping the resort going. Often their regular clothes included sorority sweatshirts, and I remember being hugely puzzled by the strange letters. As a small boy, I was having a tough enough struggle just learning to read English. Greek was well beyond my comprehension. The impact was positive, though, as I gathered that learning was important to these people, and when done well it was recognized and rewarded. That lesson never left me. I knew that one day I would go to college, too; that is if I could ever make it past elementary school.

If my siblings and I liked these girls, as we almost always did, a mutual banter of gentle teasing and practical jokes would begin in June and grow throughout the summer. For example, whoever's turn it was to clean cabin #12, the farthest from the main lodge building, would usually usurp the red Radio Flyer wagon we little boys saw as our property. Chris and I would often wait until the coast was clear and swipe the wagon back. This was, of course, never appreciated because of the long walks and heavy armloads of bedding and cleaning supplies it created. We were not terribly naughty, however. Mom or Dad would lower the boom on us long before things got out of hand. Moreover, it just felt right to be on good terms with people you saw every day and with whom you sat down to share every meal.

I remember getting along well with an amiable soul we all called Pooh. Pooh's real name was Anna, and the nickname had been a part of her since her childhood. She came to work for my parents one summer recommended by a mutual friend. She was a cheerful individual, and her good humor was contagious. Thanks to Pooh's positive influence, I overcame my fear of the dark and began to pay greater attention to the wonders of the night sky. This was at a time when satellites were becoming more common but were still novel enough to make you want to watch for them after dark. Spotting a tiny marvel blinking its steady course across the heavens fascinated us both.

It was the dark, tight, confining places that spooked me the most and sparked in me the heebie-jeebies I so wanted to purge. If Pooh spoke the truth, there was nothing in the dark that was not there in the light except in my imagination. I felt the need to test this. The basement of my family's cabin home served as the laundry facility for the lodge. A huge set of linen cabinets lined the far wall opposite the door, and I had the crazy notion to explore the small niche between the wall and the back of these cabinets.

Having entered the basement before anyone else arrived, I squeezed in behind the cabinets and let my eyes grow accustomed to the dark. Once I put aside all anxious thoughts regarding cooties and the boogieman, I found this an exciting place rich with the pleasing, fresh sent of clean linens. All my senses seemed spiked. I heard the whine and slam of the screen door when Pooh came in to start her laundry chores. Before long I could feel the heat from the ancient gas-fired mangle she used to press bed linens and table cloths. This heat was in perfect contrast to the cool concrete wall immediately behind me. There was a steady rhythm to Pooh's actions, which the loud squeal of the mangle's large, padded roller underscored. Perhaps I should have coughed or called out to make my presence known, but I was not really spying on anyone. I was there to purge, to experience, and to prove to myself that the dark actually did have something to teach if I would only permit myself to attend.

I waited quite a while in silence, which for me at that age was a triumph in itself. I did not sneak out again until the bell rang for lunch and I was certain I was alone in the basement. Afterwards, I no longer ran from the kitchen to our cabin at bedtime. I took my time, smelled the night air, looked for luna moths on the porch screen, and paid attention to the night sky. Chris still ran. Pooh's assertion about the dark was disproved a bit the night Chris ran out of the kitchen and plowed straight into a black bear raiding the garbage cans. My brother and the bear took off in opposite directions. Chris came back into the kitchen hardly able to speak. I would never have figured there was enough hair on his crew cut head to stand on end, but there certainly was. He looked like a giant version of something the Fuller Brush Man delivered.

Pooh and the other summer help stayed in the large, two-story frame structure my family always referred to as the annex. The annex stood behind the main lodge building at Gateway and was situated between the lodge and the lake on the east side of the point. This was one of the oldest buildings on the entire property. It had about eight small bedrooms, a large screened-in sun porch, and a second floor deck area. As the building was on ground lower than the lodge, a catwalk ran from a set of stone steps directly to the second floor deck. The door to the deck served as the main entrance.

The annex was originally designed as guest accommodation for sport fishermen. Spartan but clean and serviceable, each small room was a considerable step up from the fish camp tents that had been used in Gateway's earliest incarnation. About once each summer when I was little, my younger brothers and I would hunt up the sole surviving tent from those early days and stake it out on the lawn next to the annex. We always harvested a couple of skinny popple trees from a grove we called the wiener stick woods, trimmed away the branches, and used the trees for tent poles. Both this old skanky canvas tent and the rooms of the annex building were reminders that simplicity is central to wilderness experience.

When Jack and Kath were approaching their early teens, they each moved over to rooms in the annex in the summer to gain a bit of independence and personal space. My little brothers and I remained in our cabin home, but I remember being grateful for the extra room.

Dad looked at the west wall of the annex one morning, and in large brown letters he read CRIHS. It made sense that Dad would suspect me of botching the spelling of my brother's name given the struggle I was having learning to read. At the time, it would have been entirely reasonable to assume that Chris and I were both perfectly capable of making a mess with a bucket of paint. Dad simply could not believe that any child of his would misspell his own name. I was the one he confronted. I was shedding tears of denial when up popped Chris. He was caught brown handed with paint on his knuckles and his shirt.

When Jack covered the table of his room in the annex with the numerous and intriguing parts of a Heathkit radio and then proceeded to put them all together to fashion a functional receiver, I was fully certain he was a genius. I was not envious, though. Somehow I recognized that these electronic pieces were of his world and not of my own. Though there were times in my boyhood when I felt that I might never fully measure up to Jack's world, in my heart I knew that was okay. I had faith that I would someday succeed in my own. Pooh helped me realize that I would one day go to college if I believed in that dream and wanted to chase it. She explained that my first step was learning to believe in myself.

A FEW YEARS AFTER OUR SUMMER with Joe and Ardis, my parents hired another husband and wife team. This pair was from Colorado. While Gwen helped Mom and Kath in the kitchen, her husband, Kyle, reshingled the lodge and remodeled cabin #3. Jack was Kyle's helper that summer, and it was from this fellow's able tutelage that Jack learned and mastered the basics of carpentry.

Although the term apprenticeship may seem a bit antiquated today, it is an apt description of what Jack and Kath experienced at the hands of this capable duo. Kyle's guidance helped set into place the foundation of Jack's future career as a building contractor. Both Gwen and Mom helped Kath on her way toward becoming a top-notch cook and baker. This became the fine experience base from which Kath later launched her own career as a resort owner and operator.

A cardboard sign tacked to the wall of the annex greeted Steve and Patty the summer they came to work for us. They were newlyweds, and they wanted a simple summer in the woods before heading off to grad school. The sign read Honeymoon Hotel. Given the condition of the building at the time, it was probably a good thing that love is blind.

"Why do I have to be so darned puny?" I lamented one morning while Steve, Chris, and I spread gravel to create a parking lot down by the old ice house. Though not a particularly tall man, Steve was solidly built. He had the muscles and the shoulders that I was sorely lacking. Steve was also gifted with a ton of insight. I was feeling sorry for myself that day. Chris just rolled his eyes and kept raking gravel. He was already beginning to pass me in both height and weight, and he had heard me whine plenty of times before.

"You should be happy with who you are," Steve replied. "Try to make the most of what you're given."

"So, how do I do that?" I asked.

"You'll find your way soon enough," Steve answered. "But if you want my two cents worth, I'll let you know a couple of things. When it comes to real strength, attitude and will power are a lot more important than muscle. Balance is more important than brawn."

He later demonstrated exactly what he meant down at the boat docks when he flipped a canoe onto his shoulders. "You see," he said. "It's balance. If I try to muscle this thing onto my shoulders, it takes a lot more work."

"I'll never be able to do that," I groaned.

"Not with that attitude you won't," Steve replied. Then he was off to portage the canoe to the other side of the point. Although it would take a while for his lesson to fully germinate in my head, I had received his central message.

Steve was the fellow who taught Jack how to drive. That task took far more patience than my dear father ever possessed. Rather than risk trashing Steve and Patty's tiny Karmann Ghia, the lodge garbage truck was pressed into service, and dump runs doubled as driver's training sessions. Our garbage hauler at the time was an old panel truck Dad bought from his brother. In its previous life, it had served as a delivery vehicle for the Lindsay Water Softener Company in suburban Chicago. The only seat in the truck was the driver's seat. Steve rode shotgun in a deck chair coaching Jack through all the fine points of keeping the shiny side up and the greasy side rolling. Chris and I no longer even considered coming along for the ride on dump runs. We were self-preservationists. Come to think of it, trips to the dump were particularly frequent that summer. Jack had a new toy.

One day the following spring, Dad was out running errands in the Lindsay panel truck when the rear axel gave up the ghost not far from Leo Creek. Dad contacted our friend, Helmer Larsen, who owned Windigo Lodge over on Poplar Lake, and Helmer was kind enough to help Dad get the truck home using his own vehicle. At the top of our entrance road out by the portal pines, Helmer gave the panel truck one last nudge. The rear axel was by then in separated pieces, and both rear wheels spun right off the truck. Dad stopped with a jarring thud just uphill from the bathhouse. When the county grader came to work on our entrance road a few weeks later, Dad had the driver push the defunct truck to the edge of the parking lot just about where the old Model A flatbed had been before it got hauled away. Perhaps this was an upgrade in junkers. Perhaps the panel truck would inspire the next generation of rug rat dream drivers just as the Model A had served Chris and me. It seemed so prophetic that the water softener company had painted its motto on the side of the truck. The white letters read: "SET IT AND FORGET IT." That is just what we did.

Dad leased a Ford pickup to get us through the summer, and Jack's world was set right once again. The truck provided the hired help with a means of getting away from the lodge for a while when the notion struck. The occasional trip to Grand Marais, down to Aspen Annie's Bar, or over to the café at Trail Center helped break up the routine. Life at the lodge could be a bit insular. Summer staff stayed connected with the outside world by means of letter writing, the Sunday *Minneapolis Tribune*, and the weekly Grand Marais newspaper everyone referred to as the fish wrapper. Radio reception was fairly consistent though the selection was limited. The only television on the property was the small black-and-white set in the living room of our home. With this we could pull in just one static-prone station from the twin communities of Port Arthur and Fort William, which combined in 1970 to become Thunder Bay, Ontario.

Most of our hired help came to us looking for some of the same peace and simplicity that drew those first tented sportsmen to Gateway Lodge so long ago. A few months of insular living in a beautiful wilderness setting provided respite and a recharging of spirits. What my family received in return was the vast richness of several unique personalities we came to know quite intimately. My siblings and I were exposed to a diversity of human histories and upbringings far different from our own at a time when each of us was still highly impressionable. There were plenty of role models to follow; some were positive, some were comical, and most were memorable.

Buoyancy

*I*n my boyhood summers, watching mallards and mergansers bob about on Hungry Jack Lake often brought me a sense of joy tinged with envy. I was particularly impressed with the way they appeared to float so effortlessly stable when the lake got choppy and the wind had more control over my canoe than I had. My own lack of mastery with a paddle was anything but graceful until I took a lesson from the ducks and stayed in the more sheltered bays. There I practiced, ever fascinated with all things buoyant.

I remember playing alone at the beach one afternoon back before I had learned how to swim. There was a large pine log at the water's edge. It had the bark removed and was smooth and painted white. Today I suspect it may have once served as a marker of some sort, or perhaps it was used to practice the woodsman's sport of log rolling. I straddled the log and was having a grand time moving it about in the shallow water pushing off the lake bottom with my feet. Suddenly I could no longer touch the bottom. I tried to paddle with my feet the way I had seen ducks paddle, but I could gain no purchase. Growing increasingly alarmed, I leaned forward; first to try paddling with my arms and then to hug the log for dear life. I was soon way over my head and in full panic mode.

Jack heard me yelling and ran down to the beach. He quickly unmoored a rowboat and headed out to collect me. As he was trying to pry me off the log and get me to calm down, Joe came puffing up to the dock moving faster than I ever imagined he could.

"Boy, for a little poop you sure got one hell of a set of lungs on you," Joe proclaimed once he saw that I was safe. "I could hear you hollering all the way down past cabin #12."

Mom was a good deal more sympathetic than Joe when I told her what happened. After she quelled my dramatics, we agreed that it would be better for all if both Chris and I learned how to swim. To that end, she provided a cash incentive. When we both could swim from the beach all the way out to the diving raft and back on our own, Mom promised us five dollars apiece. We had to practice together.

Kath could swim, and she tried to teach us the dead man's float. After my incident with the drifting log, I probably would have picked up on what Kath was modeling a whole lot quicker if the technique had a less gruesome title. Chris and I took turns dog-paddling around the boat dock holding on to a partially inflated beach ball. Then, one fine day neither of us needed the ball to keep afloat. The two of us kept practicing until we both were sufficiently confident that Mom was going to part with what we considered some serious dough. Dog-paddling out to the raft and back to show off for Mom, we more closely resembled a couple of underpowered tugboats than the sleek Tarzans we imagined ourselves to be. Though style may have been lacking in our performance, collection was mighty sweet.

Having become more in tune with my inner duck and my own level of buoyancy, I swam often and felt at home around water, drifting logs notwithstanding. I once gathered all the Hilex Bleach jugs I could find in order to build a raft to cross the lake. My initial design was a cumbersome mess and was soon abandoned. Then I had the sort of inspiration that can only come from a glass of milk and a handful of Mom's cookies. I began collecting the plastic bladders from the milk dispenser we had in the lodge kitchen. We went through about an ocean and a half of milk each summer, and that meant an awful lot of empty milk bags. When rinsed out and filled with air, they were about the size and shape of a good bed pillow. The trick was making certain to cap off what had been each bag's dispenser hose. A good knot would do, but finding the plug that originally sealed the bag was infinitely better. When I roped a bunch of these bags together and grabbed a canoe paddle, Old Man Noah had nothing on me.

Then again, what did I really know about Noah, gopher wood watercraft, or cubits anyway? What I had created was nothing more than a fun swim toy, which was rather tough to steer. As for crossing the lake, it was probably a hidden blessing that the wind would not permit me to get more than a few dozen yards past the dock. The rocks along the shore between cabin #2 and cabin #3 became my own Mount Ararat, and from there I waded back to the beach.

When not occupied with scullery chores, my time was largely my own. I could usually be found down at the lake in, on, or around the water. The summer Pat was born, Mom and Dad asked me what I wanted in addition to a brand new baby brother for my tenth birthday. I asked for and received the privilege to use one of the aluminum fishing boats and a three-horse motor anytime it was not rented out to one of the guests. I treasured this new freedom and explored Hungry Jack Lake pretty much at will.

I learned over the next couple summers that an outboard motor is true blessing on a windy lake and a true curse when it conks out just far enough away from home to set you up with a long stint of rowing. To Dad's dismay, I built my own history of dinged props and sheered pins trying to get a boat and motor into places where they were never meant to be. This was done all in the name of discovery, and I discovered there lived within me a deep affinity for wild places. Inside me was a wellspring of curiosity for nature my early school days had never fully tapped. Putting the three-horse temporarily out of commission for the sake of exploration seemed a small price to pay. Besides, I had at least one family member with the mechanical skills to set things right once again.

Chris and I once had to go diving for an outboard motor in about twelve feet of water after a lodge guest failed to sufficiently secure it to his boat transom. Somehow the idea of employing the safety chain, which dangled from the motor, had fully escaped this unfortunate fisherman. He was grateful after our retrieval. He was amazed after Chris, not yet in his teens, tore the motor apart, dried it out, and got it running once more. All this may have been an omen of my little brother's future with marine engines.

Though I loved being out and about in a boat, it was the silence and the portability of canoes that won my heart. I recall a regular lodge guest of long-standing named Doc Keesey, who appeared to have found the ideal watercraft combination for exploring Hungry Jack Lake. He fished from a thirteen-foot Grumman lightweight aluminum canoe with an electric trolling motor affixed to a side mount. With a fishing rod in his hand and his body blocking any view of the motor or side mount, Doc appeared to be soundlessly ghosting upon the water. This was a startling sight to those unaware of his outfit. Doc's little canoe was the first I ever portaged successfully. When I was twelve, he let me carry it from his car down to the beach at Gateway making it abundantly clear that it was always to be babied. The yoke felt just right and the load was nicely balanced. I wished Steve could have seen this small triumph.

I remember well watching canoe flotillas out on the lake. As each passed, it took no great genius to figure out which groups were rookies and which groups were comprised of well-seasoned paddlers. A cacophony of wooden paddles striking aluminum gunwales always announced the former type. Theirs would be a zigzag course with invariably one or two loud stragglers. The latter type was a fine thing to behold characterized by a cadence of precise strokes, a straight course, and, more often than not, singing. Such a sight made me wistful and hungry to go exploring. Once again I lamented the sad truth that mine was not the body of an athlete. I was skinny, short, and round-shouldered as I entered adolescence. It would not be long before I started wearing hand-me-ups from my younger brothers.

My journey toward becoming happier with the fellow I was and making the most of what I was given got a major boost from a long series of events initially sparked one evening from a Canadian television advertisement. This was an odd commercial showing a fellow wearing a tuxedo standing on a high dive platform pouring maple syrup into a swimming pool and preparing to dive into it. That got my attention. Canada was soon to have its centenary birthday. The caption below the overly dressed diver asked the television audience what they planned to do to celebrate.

I did not have a clue, but Dad had an idea starting to take shape. Gateway Lodge was a mere four miles south of the Canadian border. Nineteen sixty-seven marked the one-hundredth year since Canada's confederation. Dad told us about a cross-country canoe race being planned as part of the year-long celebration. Eight of the ten Canadian provinces and the two territories were to have teams in replicas of voyageur canoes. They would paddle from Rocky Mountain House in Alberta all the way to the site of Expo '67 in Montreal. We later learned that the canoe brigades would take a slight detour from the border route and pass through West Bearskin Lake—right next door to Hungry Jack. This was a concession made to those of us Yanks eager to witness what we could of the event. West Bearskin Lake had road access whereas much of the border route did not.

Following media announcements and reports from the Gunflint Trail grapevine, Dad piled us into the station wagon and drove us over to a site where we could watch the canoe brigades pass without getting in their way. Each canoe rocketed past. When the paddlers piled out at the landing to portage to Clearwater Lake, it dawned on me that these were not the beefy gorillas I had previously envisioned. Yes, some were quite burly, but several were compact and spry. It took balance and precision to move such a heavy craft with that kind of speed. Moreover, when these guys were ashore and had to flip the canoe onto their shoulders to trot across the portage, their timing was impeccable. They continued to move as one fluid unit.

I later learned that Kath had an encounter of her own with one of these latter-day voyageurs. She had gone up to the stairway portage between Rose Lake and Duncan Lake in a canoe with a couple of folks from the lodge. She brought with her cake and beverages for the brigade members. Kath and her canoe mates were near the shore when one particularly spry and playful fellow jumped from his team's canoe right into the middle of Kath's craft seeking the treats proffered. The fellow's suddenness and catlike balance spooked my sister right out of her socks, and she quickly handed over a pan of cake to this human spring with his ridiculous grin.

Once home again, I began reading up on voyageurs and the fur trade. I was delighted and amazed to discover that brigade paddlers were typically small in stature lest they take up too much room in a canoe. Here was hope for the little guy. I knew full well that I was never going to be a star player for any football or baseball team. With my lack of height, basketball was completely out of the question. Organized athletics never really appealed to me anyway. Sure, I could see the moral value in teamwork. It was the consequences of competition that disquieted me. Why did someone have to be a loser in order for another to feel like a winner? From an early age, I have preferred competing against myself and targeting personal improvement to slaughtering an opponent and rubbing his nose in the loss. Others could keep and enjoy the typical team sports. As for me, I was going to be a paddler.

So, to that end, I began spending less time in a motorboat and more time in a canoe. There was much I needed to learn about balance and control, but I was not impatient. Besides, this was a solitary process for me with no one barking from the sidelines and no ridicule save that which came from my own voice when I struggled against the wind. I learned early on that when paddling solo in a large canoe, it is best to move to the bow seat and turn around facing the stern so as to become more centered in the craft. It took me a while longer to learn how to compensate for wind in my face.

I found myself trapped in the bays of Hungry Jack Lake on several occasions waiting for the wind to abate so I could paddle home. There was always a blessing in this, as wind kept the mosquitoes from having their way with me. Waiting out the wind gave me time to think. I figured I had better bone up on my skills as a sterns man and maybe learn a bit about sailing to boot. A fellow from one of the summer homes who had outfitted his canoe with a slick sailing rig inspired me.

Building a jury-rigged sail and mast and fitting it to an aluminum canoe consumed my free time for a couple of days the summer I turned fourteen. I was on my own with this. Chris had made friends with a kid named Joey, who lived down the lake at his family's summer home, and he spent most of his time away from the lodge running around with him. Joey's family had a real sailboat. Why was Tim dorking around with all this stuff anyway?

Whatever answer I might have given would likely have left my brother unsatisfied. Chris moved with far greater ease around people than I did, and I had given up trying to compete with his friends for his time and attention. It stung a bit from time to time, but I was beginning to realize we were separate individuals quite different from one another in ways that were beginning to matter. As for dorking around with a sail rig, I gathered the materials to fashion my own answer to *Bluenose* from the demolition of the annex building. That summer's handyman, Craig, and I were tearing down the annex, as it had become somewhat unsafe and a bit of an eyesore. Cabin #1 and Cabin #2 were relegated to staff housing. Perhaps somewhere inside his own person Chris harbored a little resentment against me for all the time I spent with Craig instead of him.

The sail itself came from a shower curtain. I swiped a long piece of quarter-round trim for the mast from Jack's remodeling project up at cabin #5. The canoe sailing rig I admired and was trying to copy had a rudder and a leeboard. This latter piece was a wooden assembly that served to provide lateral resistance the way a dagger board or an extended keel does on a sailboat. Its two wide boards could be raised and lowered into the water on the sides of the canoe as conditions required. I figured my canoe paddle could be my rudder. This leeboard contraption, though, had me scratching my head. I could probably have done just fine without it save for my need to have some way of securing the mast. I had noticed the mast on the rig I was ogling set neatly into a fitting on the floor of the canoe. Dad would likely have scalped me if I made any permanent modifications to the canoe I was using.

From the annex demolition scrap pile, I gathered a few wide planks and hammered together a leeboard contraption of my own. One short plank was set to extend downward on each side of the canoe near the middle and was joined to a narrower board that ran across the canoe near the center thwart. I drilled a hole in this top board and set my mast into it. I had to find a way to keep the mast from wobbling while making certain the leeboard was stable.

By definition, a jury-rigged apparatus is made from the materials at hand. Craig and I had just knocked down the annex chimney. We had bricks galore. Some of the bricks had holes, and I gathered enough of these to fashion both a base for my mast and a means of stabilizing the leeboard. My final result was butt ugly, as Chris and Pal Joey were quick to note. They laughed and did not stick around to watch me launch.

Ugly or not, my contraption worked. I was soon off heading out across the lake toward Mount Anna and having a blast. The sail was pulling hard. I countered with my canoe paddle under one arm and a rope in my teeth. My goal was to try to figure out firsthand what it would take to tack against the wind. I was pretty confident I could master this given enough sailing time. I was clipping along pretty well, smiling and wondering if Chris was watching from Joey's dock.

Then the mast snapped in two.

Things happened quickly. I had been leaning far to the opposite side of the sail the moment everything collapsed. The canoe almost capsized, but I was able to crouch low and counterbalance. When I first set sail, I was not hugely concerned about flipping the canoe. I learned previously by playing around in shallower water that it would never sink. Besides, I wore a life jacket. All of the bricks would simply go to the bottom of the lake if I did capsize. They were expendable. Maybe my pride was expendable, too.

My leeboard was of little help as far as stability went, but it did slow the craft. Keeping my weight to the center of the canoe, I stowed my paddle. Then I quickly stepped over the mess of bricks and boards, worked my way towards the bow, and turned around. Remaining on my knees to keep a lower center of gravity, I grabbed the sail from out of the water and put it and the broken mast on the floor of the canoe. I then reached for my paddle and slowly turned the canoe towards the shore at the base of Mount Anna.

Once on shore, I detached the leeboard and set it in the canoe with the rest of my rig. As I had done so many times before, I was back to waiting for the wind to abate. It took awhile to paddle back to the lodge. I remember hoping Chris and his friend were off somewhere distant and had not witnessed my little mishap. Then I started to think about a different kind of sail. Perhaps I could fashion a square-rigger or something similar from the plastic sheeting and the wooden frames we used in the winter as storm windows. I wondered how a fellow might fasten something such as this to a canoe.

When finally back at the lodge, I gathered up the ropes and put the canoe away. I then quietly stacked the bricks, knocked the boards apart, and gave my shower curtain sail a new home in a trashcan. The bears could have it. After sawing the jagged ends off what remained of my mast, I cleaned up the two lengths of quarter-round trim and then surreptitiously returned them to Jack's stock of lumber. Humbled but not entirely defeated, I began to look forward to putting my new sailing idea to work. I then washed up for supper and readied myself to do battle with the evening's mountain of dishes, chuckling in a bittersweet manner at my inner idiot.

I never did get around to fashioning a square-rigger. As recompense for hours spent on dish detail and days spent helping Craig tear down the annex, Mom and Dad surprised me with the gift of an August canoe trip. They had contacted a private youth camp, which specialized in canoe trips in the Boundary Waters Canoe Area and in Ontario's adjoining Quetico Provincial Park. I was all signed up for a two-week trip the camp offered paddling the Hunter's Island route through the Quetico. With just a few weeks until my fourteenth birthday, I would be the youngest in a party of six canoeists. My spirit was buoyed mightily with joyful anticipation. My backyard was about to grow a whole lot larger.

Learning to Read the Water

The first lessons I ever received in running white water included the admonition that no paddler ever drowned on a portage. When in doubt, get out and scout. Before the adrenaline rush can take hold of one's senses or the current can take hold of a canoe, it is always best to aim for the V in the river. This is the trough where the water is usually deepest and the current most swift. If the arms of the V are upriver from the point, consider this your gateway and proceed. If the point is upstream and the arms fan out below it, haul out of there, for you have an obstruction that can easily spoil all of your fun. Had I been able to step out of the flow of my days and scout around beforehand, the obstructions in my path, if not avoidable, would have been considerably less brutal.

Right about the time adolescence came knocking at my door with its packsack full of hormones, I began living for my summers and for the chance to be out once more exploring the canoe country to which my family's resort truly was a gateway. I felt at my best socially when out camping and paddling, for I could play to my strengths and my keenest interests associating with others of similar ilk one small handful at a time. The forest was my comfort zone, and I discovered there was enough of it to keep me joyfully paddling forever. Left to my own devices, I might easily have become a woods hermit retreating to a solitary log cabin or a tarpaper shack somewhere well off the grid.

My parents believed that the art of growing up was by definition multi-faceted. Because of this, my siblings and I were already being exposed to broader horizons by the time I reached my early teens. Our

70

cabin home at Gateway Lodge had become tight quarters indeed, and this was never so true as during the winter months. We rented a large house on the shore of Road Lake just a half-mile from the Gunflint Trail the winter after Pat was born. The extra space was a welcome blessing, and we were still close to our old stomping grounds. This turned out to be but an intermediate step, and before long my parents were casting about for an entirely new way to pass the winter months.

Many of the friends Dad had grown up with in Chicago had relocated to southern Florida, leaving the Snowbelt behind for good. My parents found the thought of a winter free from the perils of blizzards, snowdrifts, and tire chains powerfully alluring. Our winter in the Road Lake house was the clincher for Mom and Dad wanting to escape seasonally to a sunnier clime. We had one doozy of an ice storm while living there, which resulted in the school bus piling into a ditch and the electricity being out for more than a week in our fancy, modern, all-electric house. Trying to heat the house with two log-burning fireplaces, using kerosene lamps for lighting, and cooking dinner for eight over a Coleman stove might appeal to a person's pioneer spirit or sense of self-sufficiency, but Mom could tell you that it loses its charm pretty fast. Early the following autumn, Dad found a substitute driver for his bus run and traveled down to Fort Lauderdale to explore the possibility of our becoming winter residents there.

When news spread that the McDonnell family was about to become a bunch of snowbirds, my teachers in Grand Marais stunned me with their good wishes. They told me how fortunate I was because the schools would definitely be much better there. I had never considered that my difficulties as a learner had anything whatsoever to do with my school or with the manner in which I was being taught. My struggles were entirely my own fault, right? It gradually dawned on me that moving to Florida would provide a chance to reinvent myself as a student in a setting where nobody knew or would care about my past failings.

Dad gave up his role as the Gunflint Trail school bus driver and became captain of the largest U-haul rental truck any of us had ever seen. We drove south with truck and station wagon both packed to the gills and moved into the spacious Fort Lauderdale house Dad rented for us just before Christmas. This would be the first snowless Christmas any of us kids had ever experienced.

Going to the beach instead of going snowshoeing over the holidays and trading a parka for a pair of swim trunks was certainly novel. Still, each of us was a bit wistful when Dad purchased a fir tree for us to decorate from a fellow at a supermarket parking lot. We had always tromped out to the forest somewhere and cut our own Christmas tree. Every Christmas Mom would remind us once more of the time Dad brought home the great little tree we found growing near a power pole on one of the summer home roads. All went well until the tree started to thaw out a bit in our cabin. Then it reeked something awful. It had evidently been hit with creosote wood preservative when linemen sprayed the power pole the previous summer. We quickly hauled this little tree back outside and later hung bits of suet on it for the winter birds to enjoy.

Our first Florida Christmas was also the first in a long while without our dog, Missy. She was a beautiful tan boxer we inherited from my aunt and uncle when they moved to Thailand with their two daughters. Mom put a couple of folded blankets at the end of my bed, and that was where Missy slept. She was an excellent foot warmer, and I grew quite fond of her. Missy was well trained and had a gentle temperament. She rarely barked, and I recall she had a great love for Mom's gingerbread men. On our first Gateway Lodge Christmas with Missy, the tree in our home was eerily ringed with disembodied gingerbread heads just out of her reach.

Dad had to put Missy down just before we left the woods for Florida. This was the merciful thing to do, as she was then quite old and had become severely arthritic. In our new winter home, the nearest dog was the ugly little ankle-biter the old lady down the street would bring over each evening on a leash so it could crap on our lawn. Getting used to our Florida neighbors took a little time.

The adjustments required of all of us when we began wintering in southern Florida appeared to take the greatest toll on Jack. He was the one most vocal in expressing his discontentment, for he was giving up the winter activities he dearly loved: hunting, ice fishing, and snowmobiling. Not many of Jack's new classmates could relate to his having run a trap line or to his having learned at the hands of a highly skilled woodsman how to skin a mink. I sensed early that Jack was merely putting in his time and counting the days until we all would head back to the lodge in spring.

Jack held no monopoly on feeling isolated. Over the next few winters, it became painfully apparent that my Florida classmates had no real frame of reference from which we could build connections to my passion for wilderness canoeing. I had no familiarity with their urban upbringing. They never called me a liar to my face, but it was clear that many doubted my credibility in my communications class whenever I spoke of bear encounters. It was clear that several were skeptical whenever I read aloud the essays I wrote about life in the woods for my English class. I felt alien and sensed that I was setting myself up to become an easy target for ridicule.

There was a definite caste system at school, and my peers were cruel to anyone hugely different. I remember a girl named Alice in one of my classes. Her family had moved in from the Louisiana bayou country, and she was immediately branded a hick. Alice had a face full of freckles and a head full of snarled red hair that looked like an outsized rusted Brillo Pad. My classmates named her Sticker Patch, and she was perpetually an outsider. Though I did not ridicule Alice, I did absolutely nothing to stand up for her or to speak out against the way she was treated. I feared the rebuke of my peers some of whom likely considered me both a hick and an outsider. Being unwilling and ill-prepared to compete with my peers on a social plane or to confront them about bullying, I kept as low a profile as I could manage. Generally, I was left to myself once other students realized I was quite good at ignoring them and simply refused to fight back when provoked.

Fortunately, my new teachers and I got along well together. They appeared to appreciate that I was different from my classmates and tried to encourage me to celebrate being an individual. I took this encouragement to heart. Throughout all of my winters in Florida, I put far more stock in the value of being unique and true to myself than I ever put into the value of conforming to fit in with my peers.

Soon after starting classes in Fort Lauderdale, I was recruited for a school choral group. The music teacher was particularly persuasive. Mom and Dad trumped my initial hesitancy and encouraged me to join, feeling the experience would help me adjust to our new surroundings. In this they were entirely correct. Another choral group member and I became good friends. We performed for the school, for P.T.O. meetings, and for local Kiwanis Clubs. All went fine until my voice cracked and became froglike and unreliable. Fortunately, this did not occur until late in the school year, and the group and I were spared considerable embarrassment.

Although I never possessed an abundance of musical talent, I discovered by being a choral group member that I had quite a knack for memorizing song lyrics. It felt good not having to rely on sheet music to know my lines. It felt even better when I could keep my peers from flubbing during performances in which we were not allowed to use sheet music. Moreover, I had learned dozens of songs to sing while paddling on canoe trips.

At Gateway, Mom and Dad had boxed LP recordings of several major Broadway musicals that we often played on the hi-fi set. I knew many of the song lyrics and melodies from frequent exposure. It was a wonderful treat to finally see on a movie screen or on stage the actual shows that went with all the music and words in my head. Wintering in Florida afforded us far greater exposure to these shows. It was also humbling to realize how far off base many of my lyric interpretations were. *Fiddler on the Roof* was my all-time favorite and the musical I bungled the most. It was all the unique names, the titles, and the Yiddish phrases that threw me. Given the nature of my hearing, however, I now think I did pretty well.

During our early snowbird years, my parents took on a series of temporary winter jobs to help make ends meet. Mom and Dad were never the type to let time weigh too heavily upon them. It was essential for them to remain busy while in Florida and also to have the freedom every spring to pack up and return to Gateway. For a while, this involved their working in positions of retail sales and in hotel management. Having someone else be the boss was all a bit reminiscent of their earlier winters working in Grand Marais. Mom and Dad managed a coffee shop in a beachfront hotel during our second winter in Florida. The job came with beach and swimming pool privileges for all of us kids, which we considered a pretty fine perk. Jack helped out after school and earned enough money to buy his first car. The rest of us saw far less of him once he became independently mobile.

The independent streak in all of the McDonnell siblings is not something we simply picked off a tree. Mom and Dad cast about for some means of going into business for themselves in Florida and found a suitable opportunity in a chance meeting with a gent named Mr. Elizondo. This fellow owned a store in a plaza in Pompano Beach near the house my parents bought. The store was a bit of a hodge-podge, sort of a south Florida version of the Old Curiosity Shop. Technically, it was a store specializing in casual lawn and deck furniture, but it was a lot more than that. A friend of Mr. Elizondo rented a corner of the store to buy and sell rare coins. An elderly couple rented space near the main entrance to sell antiques. Mr. Elizondo spent most of his time working in the post office substation he fashioned in the back of the store. Mom and Dad met him at a time when he was eager to have someone else take over his furniture business.

My parents made a good team in that they were blessed with creativity as well as considerable business acumen. They struck a deal with Mr. Elizondo and purchased his furniture business, while he kept the post office substation. With six offspring to their credit, Mom and Dad figured they knew quite a bit about baby furniture. They added a full line of cribs, high chairs, strollers and the like to their inventory and specialized in serving the wee world. They also stocked a good number of rental rollaway beds. This was a shrewd move. South Florida at the time was full of retirees. Jack considered it an elephant graveyard for old fogeys. Many of these folks were doting grandparents, who could never do enough for their grandchildren when they came south to visit. My parents' store catered to their nesting needs and was quite successful.

Mr. Elizondo showed kindness to our family in many ways. He often helped with deliveries when my folks were short-handed. By May of 1970, the furniture business was far too much for my parents to leave for the summer months. Mr. Elizondo and Dad kept the store going while Mom and us kids returned to Gateway. I knew in the back of my mind that this would be a short-lived arrangement. My parents could not continue running two businesses at opposite ends of the country. However, I did not want to even imagine the possibility of our permanently leaving Gateway Lodge and the good woods. It was hard enough just to pull away at the end of each summer. Selfishly, I did not want to consider ever having to give up my summer canoe trips. Jack was less than halfway into his college career. Kath was just about to embark on hers. Both were enrolled at colleges in Minnesota. As bright and skilled as my two older siblings were, neither was prepared to take over management of a wilderness resort. I was not hugely adept at reading the waters ahead of me, but I knew something had to give.

Perhaps in crossing the country twice each year Mom and Dad took their cues from the migrating waterfowl we so much enjoyed watching. Far greater minds than mine have pondered how ducks and fish find their way back to home waters. I figured they all must have some sort of God particle inside that guides them back to where they belong. I was certain such a thing existed inside of me. I often wondered if animals sensed in their homecoming anything akin to the joy I felt when passing once more beneath the portal pines and returning home to Gateway.

In Sickness and in Health

y the summer of 1970, I had four sessions at canoe camp under my belt. I had just come off a nine-day paddle trip in the Boundary Waters Canoe Area when news struck me that my parents were seriously considering putting Gateway Lodge up for sale. A fellow I had met the previous summer at canoe camp pulled into the lodge driveway, greeted me, and asked if he could talk with Mom about real estate. I thought he was joking. The Gunflint Trail scuttlebutt had gone past my ears completely, but apparently he picked up on it. This fellow was a recently married teacher up to do a little canoeing in the area with his bride. Mom gave him a tour of the lodge, and they spoke for a while. I questioned Mom the minute he left. She leveled with me. It was now costing considerably more to keep Gateway going than it was generating. Though the lodge was not officially on the market, word had spread that our selling out would eventually have to happen. Both she and Dad were in agreement about this. My acquaintance from the canoe camp would not be a buyer, but if the right buyer were to come along, my parents would sell.

Some voice inside of me gave warning not to push Mom too far. I knew full well how hard she was working and that she missed Dad. Mom did not need my anger or sullenness. She needed my cooperation. So, I stuffed my feelings as best I could when I was around her and stayed busy. On the inside, however, I was beginning to rage.

Before I had time to give voice and clarity to my own hurt and sense of loss regarding the lodge, Mom had the chair kicked out from under her. A telephone call came informing her that her father, Charles

Leverett Hyde, had passed away. The next day was my brother Pat's fifth birthday. Mom was simultaneously dealing with her grief, delegating a myriad complex lodge responsibilities, and preparing to make a quick dash to southern Iowa for her father's funeral. For Pat's sake, she struggled to keep up some semblance of cheerfulness. Then she got another telephone call. This time it was from a family friend in Florida. Dad was in a Fort Lauderdale hospital having just suffered a brain aneurysm.

It is in times of true crisis that you discover who your angels are. When Mom learned the severity of Dad's condition, she canceled her trip to Iowa and asked Jack to drive her to Duluth. There she caught the first available flight to Fort Lauderdale. In a telephone exchange with her younger sister about the funeral she had missed, Mom received a most generous offer that helped take a world of worry off of her shoulders. My aunt and uncle had driven from New Jersey to the funeral in Iowa with their two daughters. They would now drive north to Gateway Lodge and collect the four youngest McDonnells. They would drive us kids to New Jersey, we would stay a few days, and then my uncle would drive us on down to Florida. My uncle had a few business engagements in the Miami area. He would arrange with his office for the time necessary to help us.

We were blessed with superb summer help at the lodge. They all pitched in with Jack and Kath to keep Gateway operating until the end of August. This meant a few guest cancelations and some rather hectic evenings in the kitchen, but it all came together through their collective efforts.

Uncle Mike, my Dad's brother, left his home in Chicago and drove down to Florida to help Mom as soon as he heard about Dad's condition. Mr. Elizondo and his wife took care of the furniture store until Mom was back at the helm. My own angel was my brother Pat. Soon after Mom left the lodge, Pat came to me scared and confused about Dad. He said he wanted to say a prayer for Dad and needed some help. He knew the table grace we always said at meals, but he figured that was not right. We talked for a while. Then he and I said an "Our Father" together and simply asked God to please take good care of Dad.

I realized afterward that Pat had just reminded me what it means to be a family. I felt a good deal less alone and less preoccupied with my own fears and confusion.

During the long drive south, I struggled to pull from my memory some clear and joyful image of my father lest he vanish completely. I did not fully understand the ramifications of a stroke, but I did know that Dad would be a much-altered man if he survived. I knew that his death at the age of fifty-two was a distinct possibility. The image I sought came eventually, and I let it linger and take root. The old annex building had a storage room somewhat akin to a large hall closet. On rainy summer days when we had little else to do, my little brothers and I would sometimes go there and haul out a big box full of Halloween costumes that Mom had made for us. We dressed up as a hobo, a prison inmate, a clown, or a lumberjack. One of us would don the derby hat Mom kept from her equestrian garb. The swallow-tail coat from Dad's old tuxedo looked huge to us, but one of us would always try it on anyway. Then we would look around for a special box of old photographs.

Mom and Dad never bothered to put together a wedding album. However, there had been a professional photographer at their wedding. We knew this because of the stack of photographic proofs stashed in the box each labeled with a watermark. The pictures showed Mom and Dad well before any of us children had arrived. They looked young, carefree, and full of fun. We giggled at the shots showing them goofing around and cutting up for the camera. One showed Mom struggling to carry Dad, as if over the threshold. Their faces beamed with joy in every photograph. That was the image I would hold on to—the obvious love in each picture.

It took a great deal of love to get through the next several months. Dad survived his stroke, but what it took from him was devastating. The long months of rehabilitation were arduous and frightful for the entire family. None of us knew for certain which of Dad's faculties would return to him in time and which were forever impaired. When he began to speak in sentences once again, it was painfully apparent that he had gaps in his memory and difficulty remaining on topic. It was as if his inner clock had popped its mainspring. One moment he seemed perfectly lucid and engaged in the present. The next he was spouting gibberish repeating addresses and names from his boyhood in Chicago. In their assistance with Dad's short-term goals, the visiting nurses and therapists cautioned that he must take his healing process one day at a time. This became a mantra for our family.

As Dad began to learn all over again how to speak, how to walk, how to perform basic self-help skills, our family dynamics changed dramatically. His stroke occurred three weeks before I started my freshman year of high school. I was the eldest child home. When you are only in your mid-teens and must assist your dad with his toileting, the father and son equation becomes considerably altered. I own up to being a particularly ornery cuss when I am a patient for twenty-four hours. Dad had us all beat in this regard by miles. He was absolutely awful for the family to deal with at times. Sometimes his frustration would be so great that he would lash out at the nearest of us kids with his cane and leave a welt. How often I have had to stop and remind myself that getting sick was neither his design nor his desire.

Mom was now our household's sole breadwinner. Many times I have marveled at her strength and wondered about her loneliness as she shouldered her struggle. That yoke must have chaffed more than a little at times. The husband and wife equation for my parents would never again be as it was. Dad would always be the dependent patient, and Mom would always be the caregiver and decision maker. It took a while, but Mom finally managed to sell the lodge. The proceeds went to pay Dad's medical bills.

Released

osing Gateway Lodge and coming far too close to losing my father was a double whammy that sent me reeling. I choked down my bitterness as best I could, but there were days when I was furious with God. How could the source of all good land two such blows upon us? His timing was awful. My siblings and I sorely needed a father's help and guidance each for our own strong reasons. My sense of identity was not yet fully formed, but I knew it was inseparable from the woods. Part of me was grateful that someone had purchased the lodge, as that greatly eased Mom's burden. Part of me absolutely loathed the new owners for taking our place. I had not met them and fully doubted that I ever would. It took a great deal of energy to feel this angry. It took even more to keep this anger bottled up inside of me. I feared I would one day erupt in some way that would send Mom into a tailspin. I could not allow that to happen.

It was a triumph for all of us when Dad passed a milestone, such as moving from a walker to a cane or from speaking one-word utterances to using full phrases. In time his mobility improved considerably. However, such was not the case with his coherence. His words became increasingly muddled whenever there was a spike in his frustration, and nothing frustrated him more than not being able to string his words together clearly. I wanted so much for Dad's wit and gregarious nature to return and to remain intact. I feared that the better portion of the man was gone forever.

Whenever I was fearful or upset as a boy at Gateway Lodge, I would usually retreat to a place of solitude in an attempt to rid myself of the uneasiness I felt and quell the storm in my head. Often this was a certain secluded moss-covered boulder close to the water's edge. Sometimes I would try to talk to God. Mostly I just sat waiting to settle inside. When I was really riled, there was a particular loop route I would take through the woods to blow off excessive steam. Starting off at a fierce stomp, there were a few times I almost wore myself out doing laps before a sense of balance returned. Jack's teasing sometimes sparked this action, and I admit to being too afraid of his size advantage to haul off and sock him in the snoot. After Dad's stroke, I found that I greatly resented both Jack and Kath for not being home to help bear the brunt of all the changes in our household. So much seemed so unfair.

The forest had always been my refuge and my pressure-release valve. Here I was in an urban community in southern Florida trying to cope with my anger, my fears, and my frustrations, most of which were direct consequences of Dad's debilitating stroke. Without the boreal forest nearby, I began to take solace from my school. This was something I had never before considered possible.

Dad had seemed pleased in the spring before his stroke that I had passed the entrance exams and was accepted into the same Catholic high school Jack and Kath had attended. After his stroke, there were several incidents where Dad seemed to think I was attending Leo Catholic High School, his old Chicago alma mater. Our conversations were strange, often taking on the semblance of a game of charades. It was as if he spoke a code the rest of us were only barely able to decipher.

Seeking some sort of normalcy, I gravitated toward certain of my high school instructors. The teachers I most admired and with whom I built the strongest connections were those most dedicated to integrating spirituality into their instruction. ˙ was blessed with a handful of truly gifted educators liberal in both their approach to education and their interpretation of Catholicism. This was a fairly equal mix of lay teachers, nuns, and priests. I found a new home in my literature classes and wondered why it had taken me so long to wise up and learn to love books. Perhaps I had never before had such a need for the escape hatch truly fine literature provides. I was still a slow reader, but I worked hard at my studies. Burying myself in my schoolwork kept my mind off the canoe country and away from all the difficulties with Dad. This calmed the fury inside of me. In time I made peace with my maker and channeled my energy to a more productive end than anger.

When May arrived, it came without the typical family migration north and the harried scramble to ready the lodge for another tourist season. Even so, half of our family managed to land on the Gunflint Trail that summer. New patterns were taking shape. Jack found work at a canoe outfitters not far from Gateway. Kath took a job at a resort run by friends of ours near the end of the trail. Not to be left out, Chris and I both applied for and received positions as work crew grunts at the canoe camp we had previously attended. Mom allowed us to go. I believe she sensed how strong a pull the forest had on her children. As my brother and I headed north, my thoughts turned to Mom. I pictured her donning an apron and once more stepping up to the range in the kitchen at Gateway preparing for yet another Chuck Wagon Night. I wondered about her own longings and sensed she would trade her present load of stress and obligations for her old bundle of lodge kitchen duties in half a heartbeat.

Chris and I relished being once again in the giant forest of our old back yard. We both came to know it even more intimately by exploring the detritus of old logging camps, paddling into favorite lakes, and getting to know new waters. Our familiarity with the Gunflint Trail area and with Grand Marais benefitted the other staff members at the canoe camp. This was particularly true whenever we were called upon to lead hikes or to help make a supply run to town. Canoe camp kept us plenty busy, and we fully enjoyed ourselves.

I became known as the more sedate one of the pair of McDonnell brothers employed at camp that summer. Chris had more than enough rowdy fun in him for the two of us. The other staff members enjoyed us both but for entirely different reasons. Released from Mom's scrutiny and from Dad's long list of needs, Chris redoubled the exercise of his play ethic. I went a different direction. After about three weeks, I got promoted and took over the position as the canoe camp outfitter. This meant I was responsible for packing food and equipment for canoe trips that ran from nine days to three weeks. I also got to spend more time teaching campers how to paddle. I had a wonderful summer and forged friendships that remain strong to this day and continue to keep me connected with the wild.

A pattern was set for the remainder of my high school years. Once released, it was not easy for this particular fledgling to hang around the nest. I found an after-school job as a grill cook at a great little restaurant in the same plaza as Mom's furniture store. The job also entailed washing dishes. Perhaps this was not so new a pattern after all. I earned money to pay my own high school tuition and to buy round-trip airfare to Minnesota each summer. The canoe camp hired me back each June, and the restaurant hired me back each September. I even managed to sock away a few dollars for college. It looked as though Pooh's words about college from so long ago were actually going to come true. Moreover, I had found a healthy portion of the self-confidence she suggested I seek.

Chris set patterns of his own and went the public school route. He chose to spend his summers in Florida working at a garage, learning automobile repair, and rebuilding a beat up MG convertible. Though not entirely the vehicle of his dreams, he did manage after several months to turn an odd collection of scrap parts into a spunky if not sleek runner. Chris gave me a ride when he first got his little beast going. His passenger seat was an upturned milk crate, for there was no room for the kind of deck chair the old Lindsay truck had. It was far from elegant, but it was fast and fun. You always love your first set of wheels. Unlike Chris, I stuck with bicycles for many years and troubled many a guardian angel with late night rides on the Gunflint Trail.

In Florida I still shared with Mom and with my brothers the duties of helping to care for Dad. Selfishly, however, I began giving school greater emphasis than I gave family, and I delved into my studies like a fiend finally earning top marks. I took as many independent study courses as the school would allow. Most of my classes had a teacher to student ratio that worked in my favor, and hearing my instructors was seldom an issue. When I was home, my mind was almost always elsewhere. Still a bit socially askew, I kept up a steady correspondence with friends from my work at the canoe camp, and I usually preferred their companionship, separated as we were by a couple thousand miles, to the classmates I saw each day at school. Surely I wasted several of the social opportunities immediately before me and most likely appeared aloof. Be that as it may, I was becoming far more secure in my own person.

Reclaimed

There was a routine to my Florida high school days, and I was becoming as much a creature of habit as Dad had been back when he had his Gunflint Trail school bus run. It is wise to be wary of any routine becoming too comfortable for too long. Some sort of trouble is always stirring. Trouble found me again one December afternoon during my junior year when I came whistling into Mom's furniture store with my schoolbooks all set to change clothes and head up to the restaurant to work. Mom greeted me with a doleful expression.

"It's good to find you in such a cheerful mood, but I'm afraid I have some sad news for you."

"Oh, what's up?"

"Margaret Nolan called me today. There was a fire a Gateway. No one was hurt, but the lodge is a total loss. It's gone."

"How?" I was unable to voice much more than this.

"The cause hasn't been determined yet," Mom replied. "Margaret told me that she and Harry saw flames from across the lake and crossed over on the ice to see what could be done to help. They knew right away there was no way to save the lodge. It was all gone in less than an hour. From what they could tell, no one was home when the fire started."

I felt the way a kicked dog must feel. I wanted to scurry away alone to someplace safe and far from any more hurt. It was a blessing that I needed to head off to work, for keeping busy would help keep me from crumbling. My mind eventually drifted to thoughts about Harry and Margaret Nolan. They were good family friends, and they would keep us abreast as further details about the fire surfaced. They lived on

Hungry Jack Lake right below Mount Anna. Their home came perilously close to going up in flames during the 1967 forest fire, and I sensed they would understand better than anyone else could what the Gateway Lodge fire would mean to my family.

The finality brought about by this fire left me feeling numb and empty for a long time. From the day Mom sold Gateway, I had toyed with a dream that somehow the McDonnell family would eventually reclaim the place, refurbish it, and make it a better resort than it had ever been. My imaginings strayed so far as to picture myself being the fellow to win the lodge back for my family and to make it my permanent home. I saw that as a pretty fine life and a way to honor my parents into the bargain. The idea of putting my own twist on what had been their dream greatly excited me. To that end, I had been in a rush to grow up and begin chasing my dreams. All too suddenly it was clear I would need to follow a different path.

I knew that fire was no stranger to many of the older resorts along the Gunflint Trail. Over the course of their decades of operation, most had experienced a cabin, a sauna, a bunkhouse, or even an entire main lodge going up in flames. A single night of lightning, a single forgotten fireplace screen, a single clogged chimney, or a single witless smoker was all it took. With all of the old log construction, one was only as safe as the most careless fellow in camp. The fire that consumed Gateway Lodge in December of 1972 supposedly started in the chimney of the wood stove in the staff dining room.

Early in the summer after the fire, I was a part of the annual guides' trip at canoe camp. This was a shakedown instructional excursion done before any of the campers arrived. Our route passed through Hungry Jack Lake, and we came in time to the old familiar point near the lake's west end. I did not have it in me to go to shore and walk through the ashes and charred remains of the lodge. This was no longer my home. I turned my head from the blackened scars and paddled hard and fast, wishing to be miles away, deep into the forest, taking succor from nature beneath a grove of sheltering pines.

My canoe trip friends helped pull me out of my funk. With their assistance I began to realize that even though I had lost my childhood home, by no means did that preclude my continuing to play in its vast backyard. After all, the whole purpose of my working at a canoe camp was to share with others the joy of wilderness experience. This joy and the skills necessary to sustain it were inherently transferable and not limited to a single time or a single place. I began to refocus on the instructional aspects of my summer job, and I took real pleasure in teaching kids how to get along in the woods.

That summer was my introduction to work as a canoe trip guide in the Gunflint Trail area. It was not without its particular struggles. Take as an example the little fellow who decided chopping up the wooden latrine box at a campsite was a great way to get firewood. His parents had chosen his time at canoe camp as a trial period to wean him off his hyperactivity medication. Dealing with homesick campers, fussy eaters, and kids seemingly unfamiliar with the concepts of group effort and sharing brought other unique challenges. Patience was the first lesson I needed to master, and I made plenty of mistakes along the way. Mostly, my mistakes resulted from responding in kind to negative attitudes. There were triumphs, also. The afternoon I roped two canoes together to make a catamaran and sailed with the five campers in my charge several miles down the length of Pine Lake was particularly satisfying. For the first time in my life, I began to seriously consider teaching as a potential career choice.

Before the summer was over, Kath contacted me to share the news that our entire family would be back on the Gunflint Trail in late August. Brother Jack was getting married. The wedding ceremony would take place at Sea Island Lodge on Seagull Lake where Kath worked, and Mom was bringing Dad and my younger brothers north for the event. Jack's bride to be was a wonderful young woman we all knew from her working at Gateway during the final two summers of my family's tenure. It seemed a fine match.

The wilderness setting, the joy of a party atmosphere, and the reuniting with old friends worked exactly the sort of spell upon Mom that my siblings and I wanted her to experience. The wedding took place on a beautiful day, and the first hints of fall color were popping out along the Gunflint Trail. Mom's time in the woods was the antithesis of her awful final week at Gateway three years previous. Harry and Margaret Nolan helped my family secure a week's rental of a cabin on Hungry Jack Lake just down the shore from their place. It was like old home week. There were plenty of people to help look after Dad, and both he and Mom relaxed and thoroughly enjoyed themselves.

The view across Hungry Jack Lake from the cabin my family rented showed a work in progress. The ashes of what had been our home for twelve years were being replaced by a structure fashioned from the repurposed logs of a dismantled Forest Service building that once stood in Grand Marais. The owner renamed his business Hungry Jack Lodge. Gateway Lodge existed only in memory.

I missed the first ten days of my senior year of high school, but the joy I had just witnessed and shared with my family on the Gunflint Trail was well worth the scramble to catch up with my classes. Within hours of returning to Pompano Beach, I had my old job back at the restaurant. From the outside, the prompt resumption of my familiar school year routine may have looked as though I had never left. However, there was a new lightness to my spirit. I was eager to begin the long process of selecting both a college and a career path. I knew that in a year's time I would be on my own somewhere far north of Florida.

The lightness within me also stemmed from seeing greater peace in Mom. I had a strong suspicion of what might be stewing in that head of hers and was not at all surprised when she let the rest of us in on her thoughts. As we were getting ready to head to Mass one Sunday morning, Mom announced she had decided the family should try to move back to Grand Marais. She was now determined to make that happen if she could find the right kind of employment opportunity, and she had already begun to make inquiry contacts. To that end, Mom asked us to pray for her. I feel confident saying heaven has rarely experienced the likes of the haranguing petitions fervently sent up by the four of us less than virtuous McDonnell brothers that day and for several weeks thereafter.

My family's exodus from Pompano Beach was made possible through the kindness of Bruce and Sue Kerfoot, longtime residents of the Gunflint Trial and the owners of Gunflint Lodge. The Kerfoots were opening a new supper club in Grand Marais right on the shore of Lake Superior and were looking for a manager. They offered Mom the job, and it seemed tailor-made for a person of her talents.

Life was moving at a pretty fair clip. Mom sold both the house and the furniture store in short order. By the end of March, I was petitioning Sister Marie to allow me to graduate six weeks early. I had all the credits required and had been accepted at Graceland College, where I intended to start classes in September. I felt I was good to go. My family would not be around to attend my graduation anyway. No sale. Perhaps in her role as school principal the good sister figured I still needed to develop the virtue of patience or that I had additional character-building yet to accomplish. I felt royally cheated knowing I would be left behind when my family headed north.

Uncle Mike had an apartment in Fort Lauderdale within walking distance to my school, and that would be my home until final exams were finished in the middle of May. I quit the restaurant job deciding to split my time between studying for exams and hanging out at the beach. Maybe this was not such a raw deal after all.

In early April, my family once again stuffed its belongings into a giant U-haul rental truck this time captained by Uncle Mike. Though but a junior in high school, Chris was already several vehicles beyond his resurrected MG convertible. His latest rig was a vintage International Scout, and this he attached to the rental truck by means of a tag-along hitch. Mom followed in her station wagon. My last view of this odd train as I waved goodbye included Tad leaning out of a window, pointing at me and laughing, "Nana nana boo boo." The little rat had no mercy in him at all.

The Kerfoots helped Mom locate a small rental house in Grand Marais that would serve adequately until she had the time to meet with a realtor and come up with a more permanent arrangement. Starting up the supper club kept Mom extremely busy. As manager, she was able to find suitable daytime chores Dad could accomplish at the supper club that kept him busy and socially active. Moreover, Dad was transitioning nicely and was well pleased with his new adventure. This new dining venue was getting a warm reception with the locals.

Once again locals themselves, Chris, Tad, and Pat all enrolled in the Cook County School System to finish out the school year. Jack and his wife, Sue, were living on the Gunflint Trail as permanent residents both employed by Bruce and Sue Kerfoot. Most certainly his parents' boy, Jack was starting to figure out a way to go into business independently as a building contractor. In the meantime, he managed Gunflint Northwoods Outfitters for the Kerfoots.

I was not the only odd duck McDonnell absent from Cook County that April. Kath was finishing up her undergraduate work as a double major at Mankato State. She planned to immediately follow this with a lengthy internship at a hospital in Cedar Rapids, Iowa, where she could earn her licensure as a medical technician. It was good to know that we both would be college students in the Midwest come autumn. However, I suspected my sister would be quite homesick for the woods come summertime.

Six weeks is no eternity, and I did manage to stay occupied without wishing all my days away. Uncle Mike was good company. When he returned to Fort Lauderdale, I was happy to hear his report of how easily the move had gone for my family. I began to view the time my family spent in Florida as a blessing, a valuable interlude that gave us all an opportunity to step out of the frame long enough to realize where we truly belonged. All my homesick winters notwithstanding, Florida was my salvation as a student providing much of the foundation for the teacher I have become.

One of the key complaints my family had against Florida was its lack of seasonal change. In Grand Marais during April, they could experience multiple seasons all in the course of a single day. My family was getting reacquainted with the north shore of Lake Superior and the ramifications of mud month. The last remnants of six months of snow were quickly vanishing. Spring runoff had the creeks and rivers churning at full throttle. The pulse of the forest had already reawakened. It was the season of rebirth and the perfect time for my family finally to return home and be reclaimed by the land.

Fires Within and Without

hen it came time to shake the dust of South Florida from my feet, I took a long, roundabout way north to Grand Marais and to the Gunflint Trail. The evening after my last exam, I said goodbye to my dear old uncle and boarded a plane for Kansas City. This boy was not about to hang around for the graduation ceremony. From Kansas City I took a Greyhound to Lamoni, Iowa. This was my mom's old hometown and the home of Graceland College. Mom's stepmother, my Grandma Hyde, still lived there. She put me up for a couple of days, and she was delighted that I had chosen to attend Graceland. Going to Graceland College was something of a tradition for Mom's side of the family. She and her two sisters had attended, as had several of my cousins. My grandmother had been a music professor there for several years. I declared myself an English major following my passion for literature. I registered for fall semester, selected my classes, and signed up for a dorm room before leaving town and making my way to friends in Minneapolis.

It felt good to be on my own making my own decisions in matters of consequence. My independent streak was getting a full workout. Still, I had the good sense to listen to the advice of people I trusted. One of these was John Edmundson, a friend from canoe camp. He gave me a place to stay for a few days until I could catch a ride north with a vanload of buddies heading to the woods for the weekend. John encouraged me to consider becoming an English teacher as a way to blend my interests into something sustainable while permitting me to keep my summers free to continue canoe tripping. He taught math at a private prep school in South Minneapolis, loved working with kids, and was an avid canoeist.

The previous summer, I rode along in the van with John and his group of paddlers to the put in spot where they would begin a three-week canoe trip in northern Ontario. Once he was on the water, he turned to me and said in a style all his own, "Hey, Tim, eat your heart out." The guy knew how to wound. More importantly, though, John knew how to inspire. He dropped me off on the campus of the University of Minnesota one morning during my stay with him and encouraged me to go exploring.

I was simultaneously enthused and intimidated by the immensity of the Minneapolis campus. The world was indeed far larger than the sixty-mile length of the Gunflint Trail, and I had much to ponder regarding my place in it. Here was tremendous scope for a person's imagination. Here were thousands of people scurrying about like so many ants. Because my family needed several more months of living in Grand Marais before I could claim Minnesota as my state of legal residence, I would have to pay non-resident tuition costs were I to attend college anywhere in the state's university system my freshman year. Graceland College could accommodate me as an English major. I would be plenty happy to spend a year or two there, but I knew that I would eventually have to transfer elsewhere if I decided to earn a licensure to teach English. The University of Minnesota would be an excellent choice for teacher training provided I could adjust to its size. It made a lot of sense to me to be starting out at a far smaller scale than what this vast campus presented. Since I could not be a larger ant for the time being, I was glad I chose a smaller ant pile.

My exploration included two must-see spots that John told me about. The first was in the Bell Museum of Natural History. Francis Lee Jaques painted some of the dioramas at the Bell Museum, and I knew his work from the books he and his wife had done together and from his many illustrations of books by Sigurd F. Olson. Jaques was an exquisite bird artist and a master at capturing the spirit of the northern wilds. I was particularly entranced by his dioramas at the Bell depicting the taiga and tundra of the Far North. This stoked the fires within me and filled me with a sweet longing. One day I would go and see these places for myself.

My second must-see location was in the sub-basement bowels of Wilson Library on the West Bank Campus. Here I found the University of Minnesota Map Library and a large red tome with the title Canadian Water Atlas. This was my key to countless rivers in the Hudson Bay watershed and in the Canadian subarctic wilds. Here was food for dreaming. There were hundreds of geological survey maps on file in this room showing far more northern rivers, rapids, and lakes than a fellow could explore in a dozen lifetimes. I spent a couple of hours with a select few of these maps tracing with my finger and my imagination possible water routes across vast tracts of northern Manitoba, northern Saskatchewan, and the Northwest Territories of Canada. I was hooked. When I finally left, I was determined that my future would involve paddling and wilderness exploration no matter what else I chose to do with my college education and my career path. No classroom or desk job would ever own all of me.

It felt good to be back in northern Minnesota and to have my family settled there, too. Being witness to the area's spring green up seemed to me to be well worth the notorious winters. I also appreciated seeing Mom so enthusiastic about her new position. Starting up a new dining venue from scratch and keeping it going took creativity, an eye for detail, and a vision for the future. With that same focus on the future, Mom found the family a great old house on a double lot with plenty of space for the extensive gardens she envisioned.

Once back on the Gunflint Trail, my summer was jam-packed guiding youth groups on canoe trips in the Boundary Waters and in Quetico Park. Occasionally I came across other paddlers with canoes sporting the particular logo belonging to Gunflint Northwoods Outfitters. It was one connection I had to the busy summer Jack was experiencing. His customers shared that they were highly satisfied with the service they were getting. That pleased me, and I hoped the young people I worked with had similar feelings about their experiences. Both of us had to deal with canoeing clientele during an exceedingly dry July. The fire hazard was extreme.

I was with a small group of junior high school boys in the eastern part of the Boundary Waters when we noticed smoke in the sky. Near evening, the sun looked as if it were bloodshot. We could taste the smoke in the air. The wind was not settling down at all. We went to shore and set up camp. Lacking a stove and not wanting to run the risk of a large cooking fire getting out of control, I decided to sacrifice our largest billy pot. We set this on rocks well away from any trees and built a small twig fire inside of it. Cooking supper took a long time, but none of us wanted to add to whatever chaos was going on to the west of us.

When the group was safely back at the canoe camp a few days later, we learned that a huge forest fire was burning in Quetico Park. It had been sparked by a lightening strike. A second blaze, referred to as the Prayer Lake Fire, had just torched a thousand acres not far from the end of the Gunflint Trail. This latter fire was caused by human carelessness. The route of my first canoe trip that summer had passed through a portion of this area. It stung to know that the area would not be as I had seen it ever again in my lifetime. That was a sting I would come to experience many times in the years ahead along the Gunflint Trail, in the Boundary Waters, and in vast tracts of the boreal forest much farther north. The forest recycling itself has its own timetable. We humans are exceedingly temporal and impatient creatures.

The route of my final canoe trip before starting off to college passed through much of the portion of the Quetico Park that had been ablaze two weeks earlier. Mop up crews of fire fighters were still working in the area. Our group spent one afternoon on Otter Track Lake dousing shoreline hot spots we noticed smoking as we first entered the lake. I wanted the kids in my charge to see this area firsthand to drive the lesson home about its fragility before we paddled on to more pristine spots.

COLLEGE LIFE SUITED ME WELL. I found an agreeable niche in academia first as a student and later as a teacher. Struggling to hear my course professors and later my practicum students prompted me to get a full audiological evaluation. The results showed I had a moderate-sloping-to-severe sensorineural hearing loss of unknown origin affecting both ears. As I had no history of trauma, sustained exposure to loud noises, or prolonged disease, the audiologist surmised that I was most likely born with this condition. I was not greatly surprised or discouraged by these findings; rather, they prompted me to acquire hearing aids and to learn all I could about hearing loss. Shortly after earning my degree in English Education at the University of Minnesota, I enrolled in its graduate program for training to become a special education teacher serving deaf and hard-of-hearing students.

The trajectory of my college life and subsequent career as a special education teacher was commensurate with explorations always farther north and deeper into the forests. Seeking longer and far more adventurous paddle trips than the canoe camp's format and logistics permitted, John Edmundson elected to set up a canoe tripping business of his own in the summer of 1976. He called his operation Pays-d'en-Haut, which is French for the upper country and what the French-Canadian voyageurs called the forests north of Lake Superior. He began to recruit former students from his school contacts as clientele and ran the business from his house in Saint Paul. After John's first summer doing this, I joined him as his co-guide on our first of several canoe trips to Hudson Bay.

On our canoe trips together, John and I maintained a keen vigilance for safety while ensuring each of our paddlers had a fantastic wilderness experience. Most left us happy and hungry for more. Both of us managed to trash a canoe or two in the process of helping our clients master the art of reading the water. We emphasized going slower than the current in white water and developing proficiency in the paddle stokes that allow a person to confidently pick apart a set of rapids, put the canoe where it needs to go, and make the run trouble-free. This was a major departure from the hell-for-leather river running John and I experienced at the old canoe camp. However, it was a great deal safer and a terrific challenge to boot. In learning to read people, I have often tried to employ a similar technique of going slower than the flow. That has served me well over the years.

My passions overlapped. I taught special education students in order to be of service to others and to make the kind of living that would allow me to paddle and explore. I spent my summers paddling and exploring in order to make the kind of life that would sustain joy. Canoe tripping helped me recover from the stress of the school year and to clear the cobs from my head so I could start yet another school year refreshed and eager to hit the ground running. I settled in the suburban Minneapolis area because that was where the work led me. All the while, the Gunflint Trail remained a secure and faithful mooring point for me.

Requiem

hree months before I got married in the spring of 1991, I accompanied Mom to what I refer to as the sundown ward of the nursing home in Grand Marais. Dad spent his final days there. Dad did not know who I was when I last saw him. He had deteriorated into a thin, boney, angular shell of his former self. I was uncertain at the time just how well I knew him. Drawing close and holding his hand, I gazed into his tired eyes hoping to find some spark of recognition. There was none. It was a though his pilot light had gone out.

My father was seventy-two when he passed away, and I was thirty-five. In the time since his death, I have often wondered what our life together as father and son would have been like if he had never suffered such a devastating stroke the summer he turned fifty-two. Had he survived well into his twilight years with body and mind intact, would we have found in each other good and welcome company? I have struggled to pull from the magic sack that is my memory some clear and defining moment from childhood where Dad and I truly bonded. To a certain extent, that is what all of these pages are for. I still struggle to bridge the divide between us even though he has been gone now for more than two decades. I lost my dad when I was not yet ready to let him go.

I wrote a letter to Dad just before my fifty-second birthday. This was in the still, pre-dawn hours following a terrific thunderstorm on Lake Superior. My tent was secure and well up from the water's edge. I had uncoiled the canopy guy ropes and placed heavy stones on their looped ends. When the storm hit and the rain began sheeting down, I was snug, warm, dry, and content to sit up and watch the splendid light show knowing it would bring me no harm. I do not know for certain that I slept or dreamt. I do know that before the storm was fully past, I felt the presence of my father's spirit so palpably and so compellingly that tears welled in my eyes. I shook as memories and emotions washed over me.

I wrote what follows in the pages of my kayaking journal taking care to make a copy for myself.

Patterson Island, July 31st, 2007

Dear Dad,

Your boy is still paddling. However, these days I move about in a kayak rather than a canoe and explore the Canadian shore of Lake Superior rather than the subarctic barrens. I want you to know that I am well. I have a good marriage and a joyful life for which I am truly grateful.

I am curious, Dad. I wonder what your reaction would be if in some way you could know the liberation Mom experienced after your passing. She came into her own when the responsibility for looking after you was finally lifted from her shoulders. Twenty years with you as a patient has surely made Mom eligible for beatification. I say that not out of anger or spite, but out of all honesty. She is and has always been an amazing, self-sacrificing individual.

Mom has been to Italy twice with Aunt Mabe. This has brought a new dimension to her cooking everyone in the family has enjoyed. Her gift shop in Grand Marais was thriving when she finally sold it and retired the year she turned eighty. The shop's success was a tribute to her good taste and good sense. The town's business community respects Mom, as well they should. Harbor Park was her pet project for years, and it took a lot to move that along from dream to fruition. You should see it now. Mom's gardens at home are her true passion and reflect the artist within her. I want you to know that Mom is well and happier than I have seen her in years.

I want your forgiveness, Dad. You deserved far greater patience from me than I ever gave. I want to remember you more as a good father and less as a bad patient. We were not always entirely there for each other even when in the same room. I give you whatever forgiveness I owe. I will remember you best of all as the fellow who dearly loved my mother.

Please be at peace now and know that I think of you often and with affection.

Love,
Tim

I do think of my father often, and I think of that powerful night on Superior's shore. When the storm clouds had all moved off to the east and my letter was finished, I retrieved a small bag of dry birch bark and tinder twigs from my kayak. All the surrounding wood was soaking wet, but I did not need a huge blaze. There on the beach I made a simple birch bark censer, burned the letter inside it, and said a blessing for Dad's spirit to rest easy.

I am grateful for whatever connection to my father's spirit and to his memory comes my way while I am out paddling among the waves or hiking along the ridges. I paddle and hike in part because he could not, and I do these things with love for him.

Regeneration

erial fire can pass through a dry pine forest with horrific speed, often leaving the charred, skeletal remains of trees standing until wind or rot finally cause them to topple. I have walked through several burned portions of the Gunflint Trail area over the past few years and through many scorched sections of the boreal forest farther north. When I do this, I look for signs of exploded seed cones, the remnants of which sometimes still cling to what is left of the tree branches. These are hopeful signs. They show that fire has done its job and seeds have been dispersed. If the fires swept from treetop to treetop and did not obliterate the precious thin layer of soil covering the granite bones of the Canadian Shield, the forest will soon start to regenerate. Please watch where you step.

I also look for the fuchsia-colored flowers of fireweed, which thrives in disturbed soil. Fireweed is a pioneer plant and often one of the first to show up after a burn. I consider it the botanical equivalent of a rainbow letting us know that the worst is over.

The long canoe route my friend John Edmundson and I used to follow from Leaf Rapids, Manitoba, down the Seal River to Hudson Bay was largely burned over in the nineteen eighties. Before the fires, the portages between Southern Indian Lake and the headwaters of the South Seal River were often overgrown and difficult to find. After the fires, they stood out like long crimson ribbons against the blackened earth. Moose, caribou, and what little human traffic there was along the portages pressed into the moisture that had percolated up from the permafrost layer sufficiently to leave indelible marks when fire scorched all the ground surrounding. Because there was more moisture in the plant life immediately atop the portages, they burned less completely turning crimson rather than black. All we had to do after the fires went through was follow the ribbons.

Camping in ash on esker ridges where we had previously set our tents atop luxurious layers of moss was one change I did not care for at all. I am uncertain if John and I have it in us to ever do that route again now that we are showing more signs of aging. However, both of us are grateful to have seen the forest in its prime and to have shared it with other paddlers. Perhaps the grandchildren of the people we guided will one day travel through this area and see the forest regenerated.

John spends less time on the water these days, but he still leads an adventurous life. He got bit hard by the bicycle bug a few years back and began devoting much of each summer to long-distance cycling. I turned from guiding youth groups on canoe trips to paddling with three adult friends. Together we enjoyed exploring several northern Canadian rivers always taking the time to fish and to become more familiar with the surrounding forests. Our mutual passion for this kind of travel was not always easy for those unfamiliar with the North to comprehend. Why would a person living in the Land of Ten Thousand Lakes need to drive for hundreds of miles beyond the northern border and then take a long floatplane ride in order to go on a canoe trip? A free spirit goes where it is most free. Many of my early canoe trip dreams found fulfillment in spades while out journeying with these three fellows. The demands of child rearing, pestering job commitments, and serious health issues eventually brought a halt to our annual excursions.

Unready to hang up my paddling shoes, my time on the water transformed itself once again. I took up kayaking more than a decade ago and began exploring the largest lake in my backyard. There is enough of Lake Superior to discover to keep me paddling until I am no longer able to move. I do not guide paddle trips here. I am typically a client traveling with and learning from paddlers half my age. It is a role reversal I have enjoyed immensely. Aging boomers who chronically despair about the future of our planet and our youth have not spent enough time around young people who paddle.

I still have family members who live on the Gunflint Trail. Kath and her husband Mike have owned Sea Island Lodge for more than thirty years. They raised two fine boys there, and while they no longer operate the property as a resort, it is still their year-round home. Their older son just finished building a house for himself near Leo Lake. Mike builds cabins for a living. He was Jack's partner in his construction business before going solo.

Jack changed career paths a couple of times over the years. He and Sue bought Harry and Margaret Nolan's property on Hungry Jack Lake in the early nineteen eighties. They turned the place into a canoe outfitters and sold out when complications from Jack's diabetes forced them to do so. Their son still lives and works on the Gunflint Trail. Jack now helps run Boreal Access, the Internet provider for Grand Marais and the surrounding area. Jack spends his time near the cutting edge of the digital age. When it comes to technology, I am a Neanderthal by comparison, but I can live with that. In all of the best ways that matter, Jack and I are of the same world.

Chris has become a success as a well-reputed marine welder and fabricator. He makes a fine living rebuilding shafts, propellers, and impellers for the commercial fishing fleet in Bristol Bay, Alaska. Largely self-taught, he is happily his own boss. Chris and his wife recently bought a house in Grand Marais right down the street from Mom's place, and it has the potential to become their retirement home. For a couple whose primary residence is several thousand miles away from Cook County, they spend a good part of each year in Grand Marais.

Tad is both a logger and a carpenter specializing in cedar log home construction. He cuts and mills his own lumber on a saw rig he set up just east of Grand Marais. His two sons are seldom far away from the forest they have known all of their lives. Because of his skills and his roots, Tad was the natural choice to head up the reconstruction of Hungry Jack Lodge after fire destroyed the main lodge building in March of 2008. A pessimist would say the lodge site must be cursed considering the consequences of three such destructive fires. I try to be a glass-half-full kind of fellow. My family, this resort, and the surrounding forest have all undergone a process of regeneration over the past several years. As hard as it is to accept at times, change is the major evidence of growth. Tad brought a smile to my face when he told me that someone had located the driver's side door of Gateway's old Model A flatbed truck and donated it to the collection of décor for the new lodge. Though faded, the words Gateway Lodge were still legible on the door panel.

Pat lives in Grand Marais and has been a member of the ambulance crew for the hospital there these past several years. After a few seasons guiding Boundary Waters canoe trips for the Kerfoots, he headed to Southeast Alaska to guide sport fishermen looking for king salmon and halibut. These days he fishes closer to home where he is better able to check up on Mom. Pat is a terrific chef. He carries on the family tradition of setting out a fine feed for hungry travelers.

Mom managed two different Grand Marais supper clubs for Bruce and Sue Kerfoot. Thankfully, the two venues were in succession and never operating at the same time. I always had a place to earn a few dollars during my college semester breaks and between summer canoe trips. Both properties had changed hands by the time I began teaching. Mom went into business for herself buying out the Kerfoots after they helped her establish the Attic Gift Shop in Grand Marais. She ran this until she retired and sold the shop in 2004. Mom is still going strong these days. Her gardens thrive and give no indication that she is slowing down.

I now spend my days writing and volunteering. I have found my service niche at a local non-profit organization that helps people transition out of homeless shelters and into households of their own. Having given twenty-nine years to the profession, I am no longer teaching deaf and hard-of-hearing students. When the time felt right to do so, I moved on to pursue other challenges and other joys. My wife will retire from teaching at the end of the present school year. We remain as we have always been for each other: she is my most delightful and most challenging pupil and I am hers. We go fly-fishing together and frequently journey north to the Gunflint Trail area. We are a good match for each other, and when on the water we always paddle in unison.

John and I have toyed with the idea of sometime in our dotage hiring a floatplane to fly us over all the lakes and rivers we paddled together in our Pays-d'en-Haut days. I am not certain if this will ever happen, but I do know that I am not yet ready to concede that my best paddle tripping days are all behind me. Before I take that last portage over to the other side, I would once again like to hike for miles along the esker ridges that border the Kazan River. I would once again like to take my fly rod and catch arctic grayling until my arms feel as though they will come off with the next cast. I would once again like to spot an arctic wolf from down wind and sneak up on it until I am less than ten yards away. I would once again like to hear the lodge bell ring signaling lunchtime and run home with my little brothers. Each of us is chewing on caramels, wearing a one-button shirt, and mighty proud of his root beer belly.

Acknowledgments

I am indebted to Virginia Marshall of Rapid Media, Canada, and to Elizabeth Jarrett Andrew of the Loft Literary Center in Minneapolis. Both provided me with a wealth of inspiration, encouragement, and excellent modeling of the writer's craft. I am grateful to Bruce and Sue Kerfoot for the decades of unfailing kindness they have shown my family. I am thankful to John and Randee Edmundson for enriching my life with their friendship and good humor.

Many fine paddle companions have joined in the journey over the years. My sincere thanks to you all for what we have shared together. I particularly want to aknowledge Mike Powers, who crossed that final portage well before his time. Finally, I would like to thank my family members. You travel with me always, forever reminding me that I am indeed abundantly blessed.